Table of Contents

Tables and Figures

ACKNOWLEDGEMENTS: I would like to thank Rita Diehl, Sylvia Earle, Judith Gradwohl, Don Hinrichsen, Alair MacLean, Boyce Thorne-Miller, Andy Palmer, Donald Robadue, Jr., Michael Weber, and my colleagues at Worldwatch Institute for their professional insights and critiques, which helped to make this paper possible. I would also like to thank Amy Arnette for her research assistance in the early going, and Sandra Postel for her support and oversight throughout the project.

PETER WEBER is a Research Associate at the Worldwatch Institute, and coauthor of two of the Institute's *State of the World* reports.

Introduction

From the vantage point of a beach or a coastal cliff, the oceans appear essentially limitless and unalterable, indistinguishable from the way they appeared thousands of years ago. Throughout most of human history, people held to this perspective, and their governments made few, if any, attempts to manage or protect the marine environment. The oceans were seen as largely beyond human influence because even the most destructive actions of people seemed laughable in comparison to the physical and biological resilience of the oceans.

Today, however, with technologies that allow us to penetrate the salt water depths, we have discovered that despite their size and imperturbable appearance, the oceans are vulnerable to the same unsustainable trends that are degrading the terrestrial environment. Rapid population growth, industrial expansion, rising consumption, and persistent poverty have resulted in levels of coastal pollution, habitat destruction, and depletion of marine life that now constitute a global threat to the ocean environment.

The most visible signs of deterioration in the oceans' biological systems are in those human industries that directly depend on the seas. Marine fishing, which supplies the world's people with more animal protein than any other source including either pork or beef, is facing a global crisis. According to the United Nations Food and Agriculture Organization (FAO), fishers are not only running up against the limits of marine fish stocks, but by overfishing the oceans, they have also decreased the potential yield of this essential food source by as much as 20 percent. And while fishers have been forced out of business in some regions, the multi-billion-dollar coastal tourism industry has also been repeatedly hit by polluted beaches, marred coral reefs, and otherwise degraded coastal waters.[1]

The overall biological systems of the oceans may be less vulnerable, but they too are threatened by degradation. The marine food web not only underpins the economic uses of the marine environment, but plays an irreplaceable role in maintaining the world's climate and biological diversity. Marine photosynthesis, which drives the global mechanism that moderates carbon dioxide levels in the atmosphere, is of particular importance in this era of accumulating greenhouse gases.

Despite the economic and ecological services of the marine environment, policy makers are reluctant to make marine protection a priority. In some ways, their lack of action continues to reflect the archaic notion that the oceans remain safely beyond humanity's influence. Discussions of biological diversity, for example, often omit or give only passing mention to marine species and genetic resources. Planners often fail to consider how developments on land will affect life in the sea. Even fishers undermine their own livelihoods by degrading natural habitat and depleting fish stocks.

Public outcries over the catastrophic spills of oil tankers, the fouling of beaches, and the killing of whales have prompted some promising actions—yet those kinds of high-profile issues are not the largest problems. Less dramatic, but more pervasive and ultimately destructive, are the slow, persistent incursions of coastal habitat destruction, the relentless push to increase the global fish catch, and the dispersed sources of pollution that ultimately end up in the sea. Unless we make the oceans a substantive part of the global agenda for sustainable development and acknowledge and confront the threats that face them, the deteriorating state of the oceans will become an impediment to sustainable development rather than a resource. As Rachel Carson put it in the foreword of the 1961 edition of her classic treatise *The Sea Around Us:* "It is a curious situation that the sea, from which life first arose, should now be threatened by the activities of one form of that life. But the sea, though changed in a sinister way, will continue to exist; the threat is rather to life itself."[2]

Ocean Systems

Since the beginning of life on earth, the oceans have been the ecological keel of the biosphere. The marine environment, stretching from the brackish waters where rivers flow into the sea to the hadal depths, constitutes roughly 90 percent of the world's habitable space. The oceans cover nearly 71 percent of the earth's surface, and their deepest trenches plunge lower below sea level than Mount Everest climbs above it. They hold 97 percent of the water on earth, more than 10,000 times as much water as all the world's freshwater lakes and rivers combined.[3]

The oceans' seminal contribution to the planet was life itself. Scientists believe that the first organisms on the planet were bacteria that developed in the depths of the seas some 4 billion years ago. These were the evolutionary forerunners of all subsequent organisms, and helped create the conditions under which life as we know it could evolve. The early biosphere was inhospitable to other life forms partly because the atmosphere was deficient in oxygen. In the process of synthesizing simple sugars from carbon dioxide, photosynthetic strains of marine bacteria created the oxygen-rich atmosphere in which more advanced life forms could develop.[4]

Since the beginning of life on earth, the oceans have been the ecological keel of the biosphere.

Time and evolution have distanced us from our oceanic origins, but we still bear the traces of our saltwater heritage in our blood. The almost universal human fascination with the timeless procession of waves, the smell of salt water, and the call of seabirds also bespeaks a deep-seated psychological connection with the oceans. Yet, without attention to those connections, we can easily become oblivious to the critical roles that the oceans play in the biosphere.

Arguably, the oceans' most important function is the regulation of global climate. Their huge mass, for instance, moderates local temperatures by absorbing heat in the summer and releasing heat in the winter. Oceanic currents further even out temperatures by absorbing heat near the equator and releasing it as they approach the poles. The Gulf Stream, for instance, transports warm water from the Gulf of Mexico to northern Europe, moderating the climate to such an extent that lemon trees can grow along the coast in western Ireland at nearly the same latitude as Moscow. Shifts in oceanic currents—a potential consequence of global warming—would bring drastic changes in regional climates. On a global level, temperatures might average between one and two degrees Celsius higher if not for the heat absorbed by the oceans.[5]

The oceans' biological processes, too, contribute to this climate-regulating function. In the process of producing one-third to one-half of the global oxygen supply, marine photosynthesis removes the primary greenhouse gas, carbon dioxide, from the atmosphere through a mechanism known as the biological pump. Carbon dioxide enters the churning upper layer of the oceans, where phytoplankton and other marine plants use it in photosynthesis to make simple sugars. While 90 percent of this carbon is recycled through the marine food web, some falls into the deeper layers of the oceans as the detritus of decaying phytoplankton and other sea plants or animals. There, the organic matter is oxidized and stored as dissolved carbon dioxide in deep ocean currents. It takes about 1,000 years for these slow-moving currents to bring the carbon back to the surface.[6]

The biological pump is the successor to the primitive process that initially created the oxygen-rich atmosphere a few billion years ago. Today, by slowing the buildup of greenhouse gases, the biological pump is credited with helping to delay the onset of global warming. The rise in greenhouse gases is driven by such human activities as burning fossil fuels and clearing forests, which release 7 billion tons of carbon (in the form of carbon dioxide) into the atmosphere each year. About half of this excess carbon stays in the atmosphere, contributing to the buildup in greenhouse gases, while one-third is taken up and retained in the oceans.[7]

The oceans are also an important link in the carbon cycle because they store more than 20 times as much carbon as all of the world's forests and other terrestrial biomass combined.

Because the oceans hold so much carbon, a disruption to the oceans' systems could not only slow the uptake, but also release additional amounts of carbon dioxide into the atmosphere, accelerating the buildup of greenhouse gases in the atmosphere.[8]

Besides driving the biological pump, marine photosynthesis is at the foundation of the oceanic systems that yield 80 million tons of seafood per year. Globally, the marine catch accounts for 16 percent of animal-protein consumption and is a particularly important source of protein in developing countries. In Asia, one billion people rely on fish as their primary source of protein, as do many people in island nations and the coastal nations of Africa.[9] (See Figure 1.)

Marine biological diversity is crucial to maintaining the health and stability of the food web and the biological pump. Organisms from bacteria to great blue whales occupy necessary ecological niches. Copepods, for instance, are minute crustaceans that eat phytoplankton and are thought to be the most numerous animals in the oceans. They fill a critical link between the oceans' primary producers and the rest of the food chain. If

FIGURE 1:

Contribution of Fish to Diet by Region, 1987–89

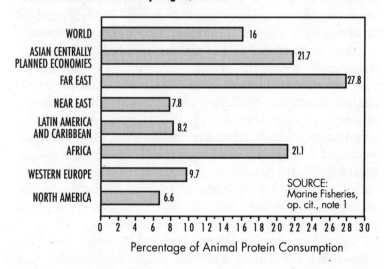

SOURCE:
Marine Fisheries,
op. cit., note 1

Percentage of Animal Protein Consumption

ecological conditions change such that copepods can no longer perform this function, their disappearance would have damaging effects unless the biodiversity of their subclass is sufficient to produce a successful substitute.[10]

In addition to its ecological significance, the oceans' biological storehouse is of global scientific importance. About 90 percent of the history of life on earth has taken place in salt water, making the oceanic gene pool an invaluable resource. Its species are the descendants of the 3.5 billion years of evolution that predated the appearance of life on dry land some 450 million years ago. Many of them have no evolutionary counterparts on land.

Of the 1.4 million species so far catalogued worldwide, only 160,000 are marine. But in the cataloging of species, it is likely that the oceans have been vastly underrepresented. Traditional wisdom has it that terrestrial habitat—and therefore the life it contains—is more diverse than marine habitat and life. Yet, because marine biological diversity is so poorly documented, the true number of ocean species is certain to be higher than so far tallied, and the relative diversity of land and sea has yet to be determined. According to James McCarthy, a biological oceanographer at Harvard University, even the best taxonomists are able to identify only 20 percent of phytoplankton in the open ocean, and as much as 80 percent of the biomass consists of these and other extremely small, hard-to-identify organisms.[11]

Furthermore, if biological diversity is measured in terms of the physical disparities between species, as classified by fundamental body characteristics in phyla, the diversity is *greater* in the oceans than on land. (Humans and bony fish, for instance, are both members of the phylum *chordata*, whose fundamental characteristic is a flexible spinal cord and complex nervous system.) Of the 33 animal phyla, 15 exist exclusively in the oceans—whereas only 1 of the 33 lives exclusively on land. Another 5 phyla are at least 95 percent marine.[12]

Scientific researchers are increasingly turning to the sea in their search for medical cures and unique compounds. They have derived anti-leukemia drugs from sea sponges, bone graft material from corals, diagnostic chemicals from red algae, anti-infection compounds in shark skin, and many more useful agents. Because marine life is relatively unstudied compared to terrestrial life, the oceans are a vast new frontier for research.[13]

In trying to understand the diversity and distribution of life on land, we observe the variations in terrestrial environments—marshes, deserts, grasslands, mountains, rainforests—that alter the basic conditions for growth and survival. In contrast, to the untrained eye, the sea may seem much the same everywhere. But in fact, ocean habitats vary radically, from glacially cold plains and mountain ranges thousands of meters below sea level, to shallow, brilliant coral reefs in the dancing light of the tropical waters.

In general, coastal waters are more riotous with life than the open ocean or the deep sea because they contain the most abundant food sources. Twenty percent of the oceans' plant production occurs in the 9.9 percent of the ocean area that lies over continental shelves. Here, microscopic phytoplankton and bottom-dwelling plants thrive on the nutrients that rivers deliver from land. Continental shelves extend an average of 70 kilometers from shore, but more extensive ones can be found in such areas as the North Atlantic and Southeast Asia. Phytoplankton, which make up the bulk of marine productivity, also concentrate near the continents, where coastal winds drive off the surface waters, allowing deep sea currents laden with nutrients to come to the surface. "Upwelling" zones, such as those off the western coasts of South America and southern Africa, cover 0.1 percent of the oceans and are some of their most productive waters. But it is where the oceans touch land that the greatest fecundity can be found; the nutrient-rich brackish waters of river estuaries, mangrove swamps, and salt marshes are thought to produce more organic material per square meter than any other habitat on earth.[14]

Because of the concentrated food sources they contain,

The biological pump is the successor to the primitive process that first created an oxygen-rich atmosphere several billion years ago.

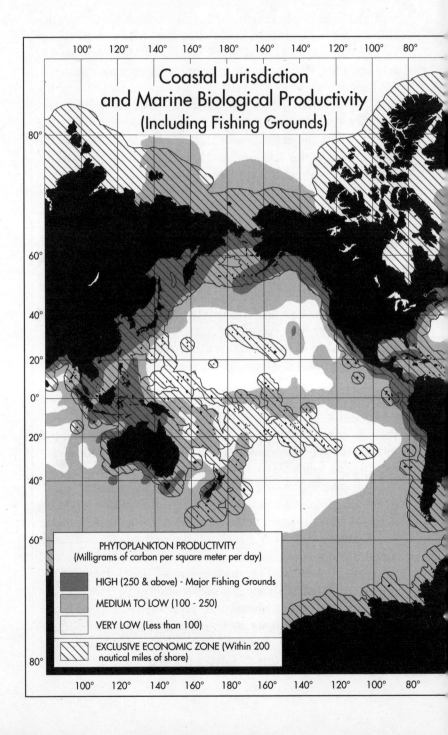

Coastal Jurisdiction and Marine Biological Productivity (Including Fishing Grounds)

PHYTOPLANKTON PRODUCTIVITY
(Milligrams of carbon per square meter per day)

HIGH (250 & above) - Major Fishing Grounds

MEDIUM TO LOW (100 - 250)

VERY LOW (Less than 100)

EXCLUSIVE ECONOMIC ZONE (Within 200 nautical miles of shore)

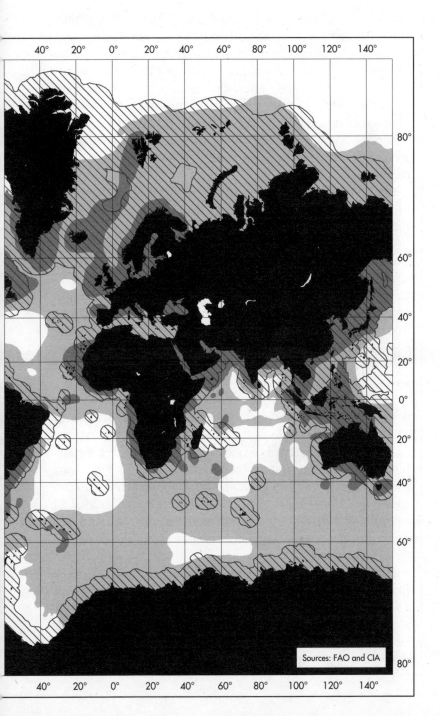

Sources: FAO and CIA

coastal waters support a high density of marine life, making them the centers of ocean fishing. The world's major fishing grounds correspond almost exactly with the regions of highest photosynthetic productivity (see map, page 12). Ninety percent of the marine fish catch comes from the third of the oceans nearest to the coasts. Estuaries and wetlands, because of their extreme abundance of food, are the nurseries for many species of juvenile fish. About two-thirds of all commercially valuable fish species spend the first and most vulnerable stages of their life in these waters.[15]

In contrast, the productivity of the open ocean has often been compared to that of a desert. While both have low plant production, the connotation of barrenness is misleading, because neither is devoid of life. The low density of phytoplankton leaves the open waters clear and blue, allowing photosynthetic activity to occur at greater depths than in coastal waters. The total mass of phytoplankton, dispersed across 90 percent of the oceans' surface, accounts for 80 percent of marine productivity. Although barren by comparison to coastal areas, the open ocean is the engine that drives the biological pump. Its food web also supports such important migratory species as tuna, dolphins and salmon, which graze the dispersed animal life there.[16]

Coastal waters, while more productive, make a smaller contribution to the open ocean food web and the biological pump. The majority of carbon dioxide captured in coastal waters is recycled, but a small percentage of the organic matter is transported into the deep waters through the chain of marine organisms that starts with copepods and other zooplankton, and progresses up to large migratory species. Unlike on land, animal life makes up the majority of biomass in the oceans, and its movement into the open ocean redistributes some of the productivity of coastal waters.[17]

Below 1,000 meters, in the realm of perpetual night, no plants grow at all. Organisms there rely primarily on the slow rain of food particles falling from above. Only at the occasional geologic fissures in the ocean floor do deep sea communities have their own source of primary food production. At these thermal vents, which are thought to be the font of all life on Earth, bacteria still consume the inorganic molecules synthesized in the intense heat from the volcanic activity below. The crabs, starfish and other organisms that have adapted to the noxious chemicals and heat of these primordial environments contrast sharply with the more dispersed and smaller life forms of the extensive deep sea floor because of the immediate source of food.

Though devoid of plants, the deep ocean is not the biological graveyard that scientists once thought it was. Remarkably, deep sea dredges indicate that the ocean floor may contain as many species as the world's tropical rainforests, generally regarded as the world's most species-rich ecosystems. Many of the species brought to the surface cannot be identified because they have never been seen before, and successive dredges are unlikely to repeat previous finds. The density of unique species in the deep ocean is not thought to be high, but because half the earth's surface is 3,000 meters or more below sea level, the total count is thought to be extraordinary.[18]

About 90 percent of the history of life on Earth has taken place in salt water.

A general rule of marine diversity is that the higher the nutrient load is, the lower the diversity of life will be. This is because abundant food sources tip the ecological balance in favor of dominant species which out-compete less vigorous species. In the open and deep ocean, the vast expanse, many layers (with their wide ranges of temperature and light), and low availability of food make room for an abundance of unique species. These waters contrast sharply with coastal areas, which contain a higher density of life, but a lower diversity.[19]

Coral reefs are a special case. These coastal ecosystems are both highly diverse *and* highly productive. They do not form in nutrient-rich waters, but in tropical coastal waters that are clear, blue, and low in nutrients like the open ocean. However, coral reefs are nearly as productive as estuaries and wetlands because they take photosynthetic advantage of the ample sunlight that penetrates the clear, blue waters, and they efficiently recycle the available nutrients within the structured ecosystem. The diverse community of coral reef species helps to maintain the ecosystem and recycle its modest supply of nutrients.

Within coastal waters, the rule of diversity can be further elaborated: shallow waters are more diverse than deeper waters, rocky areas are more diverse than sandy or muddy ones, and the tropics are more diverse than temperate or polar zones. Shallow, rocky, tropical—and nutrient-poor—coral reefs, not surprisingly, are believed to contain the highest density of unique species in the oceans. For the world as a whole, the heart of coastal biological diversity lies in Southeast Asia, with decreasing diversity spreading out into the Indian and Pacific oceans. The Caribbean Sea is the center of coastal biological diversity for the Atlantic Ocean, and among the world's systems ranks a distant second behind Southeast Asia.[20]

While distinctions between regions of the ocean are instructive, they can obscure the underlying interdependence of the marine environment. Nutrients cycle from the coasts to the deep ocean and back, species migrate between continents, and—over the eons—the biological miracle of the deep thermal vents continues to build the genetic diversity of the oceans. The oceans are even connected, like a single global organism, by great currents that slowly flow from hemisphere to hemisphere. The essential value of understanding these interconnected systems is to provide a means of protecting them—and ourselves—from degradation of a magnitude we can barely imagine.

Living on the Edge

If we were to declare war against the oceans, the most destructive strategy we could devise would be to target the coasts, the regions of most highly concentrated biological activity. Tragically, that is what human activity is already doing—not by deliberate attack, of course, but through overcrowding of coastal areas and unsustainable economic development. Because the oceans' vital processes are heavily concentrated in coastal waters, disruptions there have a disproportionate effect on the whole ocean ecosystem.

These waters are under the greatest environmental stress

because the coasts are the natural crossroads between human activity and the sea. Here is where agricultural and urban waste flows in from the land, smoggy clouds pour out their contaminants, ships flush their tanks, and cities bulldoze wetlands to extend their land seaward. Some of this pollution and habitat destruction spills over into the open ocean and threatens the marine environment through the global phenomena of stratospheric ozone depletion and global warming. But because of the immediate threats to the coastal waters, a high proportion of marine degradation is found there.

Of the total pollution load entering the oceans worldwide, about three-quarters comes from human activities on land. (See Table 1.) Ironically, human industries and settlements are choking the oceans with the very rivers that make coastal waters productive. The majority of nutrients, sediments, pathogens, persistent toxins, and thermal pollution all come from land-based sources. Even oil pollution, which is typically associated with accidents at sea such as that of the Exxon Valdez, actually comes as much from land as from sea sources. Only the introduction of alien species (genetic pollution) and noise pollution originate primarily from sea-based sources. (See Table 2.)[21]

The flow of nutrients into the oceans has at least doubled since prehistoric times, and sediments have nearly tripled as a

TABLE 1.
SOURCES OF MARINE POLLUTION

	(Percentage by weight)
Run-off and discharges from land	44
Airborne emissions from land	33
Shipping and accidental spills	12
Ocean dumping	10
Offshore mining and oil & gas drilling	1
All Sources	100

Source: GESAMP, *The State of the Marine Environment,* op. cit., note 21.

TABLE 2.
MARINE POLLUTION

Type	Primary Source/Cause	Effect
Nutrients	Runoff approximately 50% sewage, 50% from forestry, farming, and other land-use. Also airborne nitrogen oxides from power plants, cars, etc.	Feed algal blooms in coastal waters. Decomposing algae depletes water of oxygen, killing other marine life. Can spur toxic algal blooms (red tides), releasing toxins that can kill fish and poison people.
Sediments	Erosion from mining, forestry, farming, and other land-use; coastal dredging and mining.	Cloud water; impede photosynthesis below surface waters. Clog gills of fish. Smother and bury coastal ecosystems. Carry toxins and excess nutrients.
Pathogens	Sewage, livestock.	Contaminate coastal swimming areas and seafood, spreading cholera, typhoid and other diseases.
Alien species	Several thousand per day transported in ballast water; also spread through canals linking bodies of water and fishery enhancement projects.	Outcompete native species and reduce biological diversity. Introduce new marine diseases. Associated with increased incidence of red tides and other algal blooms. Problem in major ports.
Persistent Toxins (PCBs, DDT, heavy metals, etc.)	Industrial discharge; wastewater from cities; pesticides from farms, forests, home use, etc.; seepage from landfills.	Poison or cause disease in coastal marine life, especially near major cities and industry. Contaminate seafood. Fat-soluble toxins that bio-accumulate in predators can cause disease and reproductive failure.
Oil	46% from cars, heavy machinery, industry, other land-based sources; 32% from oil tanker operations & other shipping; 13% from accidents at sea; also offshore oil drilling and natural seepage	Low-level contamination can kill larvae and cause disease in marine life. Oil slicks kill marine life, especially in coastal habitats. Tar balls from coagulated oil litter beaches and coastal habitat. Oil pollution is down 60 percent from 1981.
Plastics	Fishing nets; cargo and cruise ships; beach litter; wastes from plastics industry and landfills.	Discarded fishing gear continues to catch fish. Other plastic debris entangles marine life or is mistaken for food. Plastics litter beaches and coasts and may persist for 200 to 400 years.
Radioactive isotopes	Discarded nuclear submarines and military waste; atmospheric fall-out; also industrial wastes.	Hot spots of radioactivity. Can enter food chain and cause disease in marine life. Concentrate in top predators and shellfish, which are eaten by people.
Thermal	Cooling water from power plants and industrial sites.	Kill off corals and other temperature sensitive sedentary species. Displace other marine life.
Noise	Supertankers, other large vessels and machinery.	Can be heard thousands of kilometers away under water. May stress and disrupt marine life.

Compiled by Worldwatch Institute; see note 21 for sources

result of human activity. Together, nutrients and sediments have become pollutants that degrade estuaries and coastal waters by prompting algal blooms, blocking sunlight, suffocating fish and coastal habitats, and carrying pathogens and toxins. Globally, nutrient and sediment pollution have contributed to the decline of estuaries, coastal wetlands, coral reefs, seagrass beds, and other coastal ecosystems. They have also contributed to the increased incidence of "red tides," blooms of algae that release deadly levels of toxins into the surrounding waters. In Japan's Seto Inland Sea, the number of red tides increased from 40 in 1965 to more than 300 in 1973.

Three years later, after the Japanese author- ities had introduced controls to limit the influx of nutrients, red tides began to decline in frequency. In other areas, how- ever, the influx continues to worsen. The poisons released by red tides kill mass quantities of fish and can weaken or kill people through direct exposure or conta- minated seafood.[22]

The coasts are the natural crossroads between human activity and the sea.

A large portion of the nutrients enter- ing coastal waters comes from the ubiqui- tous problem of city sewage. Eutrophying nutrients, however, are only part of the trouble brought by this waste. Sewage sludge at concentrations as low as 0.1 percent is toxic to herring and cod eggs. Untreated sewage—including overflow during rain storms—threatens the health of unwitting swimmers and con- sumers of contaminated seafood. Cities also commonly mix wastewater from small industries with street runoff and sewage, thereby contaminating the water with oil, heavy metals, and other health- and environment-threatening toxins.[23]

A surprising proportion of the pollutants entering coastal waters originates not from the adjacent coastal land but from more distant sources. Of the nutrients, at least half come from inland. In the eastern United States, for instance, the Chesapeake Bay has been overwhelmed by nutrients from distant sources. Farmers contribute one-third and air pollution another one- quarter of the nitrogen pollution that has contributed to the decline of this estuary, the largest in the United States and once one of the most productive in the world. The oyster catch in the Chesapeake fell from 20,000 tons per year in the 1950s to under 3,000 tons in the late 1980s, at least partly as a result of pollution. When Europeans first came to the United States, oysters in the Chesapeake could filter all the water in the Bay in two weeks. Now, because there are so few, they take more than a year.[24]

In a study of 42 of the world's major rivers, Jonathan J. Cole and his colleagues at the Institute of Ecosystem Studies at the New York Botanical Garden showed that the level of pollution correlates uncannily with the level of human activity in the watershed. The Rhine, for example, has ten times the population density of the Mississippi, and dumps ten times more nutrients into the sea, even though the Mississippi drains an area 14 times larger.[25] (See Figure 2.)

The vulnerability of the oceans' health is demonstrated by their sensitivity to nutrient levels. Thus, a nutrient flow that is too low can be as detrimental to estuaries and other coastal ecosystems as one that is too high. When the Egyptians closed off the Aswan High Dam at Lake Nassar in 1965, they cut off the flow of nutrient-laden sediments into the Nile Delta. The following year, phytoplankton concentrations fell by 90 percent, and the sardine catch dropped precipitously, from an average of 18,000 tons per year in the early 1960s, to 1,200 tons in 1966, and then 600 tons in 1969. The data from the Cole study show that the Nile now exports far smaller amounts of nutrients than other watersheds with similar population densities.[26]

About one-third of the pollutants entering the marine environment come from air emissions, a large portion of which settle into coastal waters. For many heavy metals and volatile organic chemicals, air is the primary route to the sea. In the North Sea, about a quarter of the pollution, including the majority of PCBs and other chlorinated organic chemicals, comes from the air. In the Persian Gulf, the 4 to 12 million barrels of oil that the Iraqi army deliberately spilled during the 1991 Gulf War turned out to be only part of the total amount of oil estimated to have entered the Gulf as a result of the war. Another

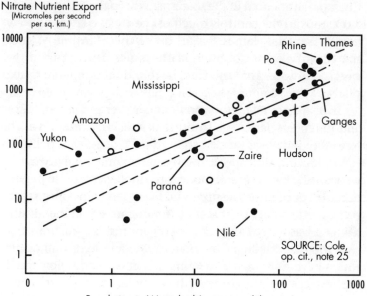

FIGURE 2:

Population and Marine Pollution From Major Rivers

Nitrate Nutrient Export
(Micromoles per second
per sq. km.)

Population in Watershed (per square kilometer)

SOURCE: Cole, op. cit., note 25

4 to 5 million barrels is thought to have been carried into the Gulf by the oil-laden smoke rising from oil fires on land. Worldwide, about ten percent of the oil that reaches the oceans is airborne.[27]

Marine biological diversity is directly threatened by the transport of fish and other marine life from one part of the oceans to another where they are not a part of the established ecosystem. These introductions of what are known as exotic or alien species constitute another form of pollution—in this case, genetic pollution. When the new arrivals out-compete the native species, they have a homogenizing effect on the oceans' biological diversity, and they can dramatically transform their new homes. Alien species can be found in coastal ecosystems around the world, but because they are not consistently monitored, these introductions and the resulting changes are poorly documented. Anecdotal evidence, however, indicates that this

form of pollution can bring major injury to marine environ-
ments. For example, the periwinkle snail *(Littoriina littorea)*,
which was introduced to the shores of New England from Europe
in the 1860s, now controls much of the rocky coast from New
York to Canada. James T. Carlton of the Maritime Studies
Program at Williams College in Massachusetts reports that in the
Long Island Sound of New York, he found moorings encrusted
with brown sea squirts *(Styela clava)* native to Japan, green algae
(Codium fragile tomentosoides) from Asia, and a Southern
Californian species of sea squirt *(Botrylloides)*, none of which
were present 35 years ago.[28]

Introducing alien species constitutes an unnatural stirring of
the oceans' gene pool, and modern technologies have increased
the speed of the homogenizer. Old wooden ships once sailed
with up to a meter's thickness of "fouling mass" on their hulls,
in which was lodged a plethora of organisms ranging from sea-
weed and barnacles to crabs and fish. Modern toxic hull paints
(which have their own environmental effects) and high-speed
ships have all but eliminated this means of spreading alien
species. Unfortunately, transport on the outside of the hull has
been replaced by even more capacious transport inside. Ocean-
going vessels take in up to 50,000 tons or more of ballast water
to stabilize them for trips without cargo. Researchers have
found hundreds of marine plants and animals that can survive
the trip to the next port, including species of toxic phytoplankton that contribute to "red tides". A study of 80 ships
entering ports in Australia found that five of them carried toxic
species of phytoplankton (dinoflagellates). Scientists studying
toxic algal blooms hypothesize that this form of genetic pollution is also a contributing factor to the increasing incidence of
red tides.[29]

According to Carlton, marine scientists find the scale and
speed of this blending of the marine ecosystems mind-boggling.
Ships entering South African ports discharge some 20 million
tons of ballast water every year, and those in the United States
discharge 56 million tons, an estimated 6,400 tons every hour.
Carlton estimates that with a world fleet of 35,000 ships, a minimum of several thousand different ballast-borne species may be

on their way across the oceans on any given day.[30]

Other disseminators of genetic pollution include canal cuts and projects to increase fish production. The opening of the Suez Canal led to the spread of more than 250 species from the Red Sea to the Mediterranean, including the now highly abundant Red Sea jellyfish *(Rhopilema nomadica),* which has depressed the fish catch, clogged the intake pipes of coastal power plants, and scared off tourists in the eastern Mediterranean.[31]

Ironically, government hatcheries established to offset damage to natural runs by dams, forestry, or agriculture can themselves drastically alter the genetic pools of the runs. In one study of a stocking project on a dammed river in Ireland, researchers found that fewer than 30 percent of the returning salmon were wild. In the western United States, attempts to augment the coho salmon run by domestic stocking reduced the number of wild coho juveniles by up to 40 percent and did not increase the number of salmon that returned to spawn. Farmed salmon also contribute to genetic pollution when they escape into the wild. In Norwegian rivers, domesticated species now make up between 25 and 50 percent of the salmon populations. The farmed species also bring diseases and parasites that infect wild populations. In the 1980s, for example, a parasite known as the fluke *(Gyrodactylus salaris)* spread from river to river and resulted in an estimated annual loss of 250 to 500 million tons of salmon.[32]

Introducing alien species constitutes an unnatural stirring of the oceans' gene pool, and modern technologies have increased the speed of the homogenizer.

Whether via dams on rivers or coastal development, marine pollution and habitat destruction often go hand in hand. To pave coastal cities, for instance, developers drain wetlands or build over other coastal habitat. Runoff from construction, city streets, and industrial facilities flows unimpeded into coastal waters where wetlands once served to trap nutrients, sediments and toxins. The world is replete with examples of cities that have degraded nearby coastal habitats through the combined effects of direct habitat destruction and pollution. Commercially burgeoning Singapore, for example, has removed almost all of its mangroves and degraded the majority of its seagrass beds and all but 5 percent of its coral reefs. San Francisco Bay, the largest estuary in the western United States, has lost 60 percent of its water area to land reclamation in the last 140 years, is overrun by alien species, and can no longer support commercial fishing. Off the Palos Verdes peninsula just south of Los Angeles, a city sewage plant contributed to the progressive elimination of 7.8 square kilometers of kelp forest as it increased its discharge 20-fold between 1928 and 1966. The toxin- and heavy metal-laced sludge covered 95 percent of the former kelp bed.[33]

Loss of coastal habitat is a global problem, now affecting some of the oceans' most productive and diverse environments. About half of the world's saltmarshes and mangrove swamps have been cleared, drained, diked or filled. Five to 10 percent of the world's coral reefs have essentially been eliminated by pollution and direct destruction, and another 60 percent could be lost in the next 20 to 40 years. Even beaches (which are not highly productive but are essential to many marine species, including sea turtles) are endangered, with 70 percent eroding worldwide.[34]

A large portion of the destruction occurs because human populations mirror the biological activity of the sea, with the highest density generally near the coasts. Over half the people in the world are estimated to live within 100 kilometers of the coast. In Southeast Asia, where marine biodiversity is particularly high, over two-thirds of the people live within the coastal zone. In China, the population density along the coast is three times as high as the national average. Coastal populations are also particularly high in southern Asia, Europe, southeastern Africa, and portions of North and South America.[35]

Coastal populations appear to be growing more rapidly than total world population. Coastal cities, which make up 9 of the 10 largest cities and over two-thirds of the top 50, are expected to grow with increasing urbanization. The United Nations estimates that 20 to 30 million more of the world's poorest people migrate from rural to urban areas each year, especially to Third World megacities. Nearly one-fifth of the world population lives in coastal cities.[36]

Poverty is a factor in the global coastward migration. The promise of employment in cities draws people from depressed agricultural areas. Coastal cities have the economic benefit of access to the oceans for trade. Cities are attracted to estuaries (natural bays and river mouths) because they make excellent harbors. Ships can freely enter from the ocean, and they are sheltered from waves. These urban areas particularly threaten the marine environment because a host of pollutants flows from city streets, industrial installations, sewage systems and docked ships, while the demand for land gives people incentive to clear and fill in coastal habitat.

Rural coastal populations may also be increasing. In the Philippines, coastal population is growing faster than in the rest of the country, partly because people who give up on farming often move to coastal areas to try fishing. While land is scarce, open access to fishing grounds gives poor people at least the hope of making a living. Although coastal cities are notorious for degrading and destroying the marine habitat around them, the most extensive source of *direct* habitat destruction along the coasts actually occurs in rural areas. Shrimp farmers in the Asian and South American tropics, for instance, have cleared extensive tracts of mangroves for holding ponds. Responding to international demand, these farmers produce 20 percent of the world's shrimp and constitute one of the primary causes of mangrove decimation. In Thailand, shrimpers clear mangroves illegally, but with apparent impunity because of the power and influence of the shrimp industry. In 1993, a Thai forest ranger who arrested would-be shrimp farmers for damaging mangroves was later shot and killed, apparently in retribution for this arrest. In ripping out space for domestic shrimp operations, such farmers destroy the natural nurseries for wild shrimp and thereby reduce stocks for offshore shrimp fishers.[37]

In similar pursuit of coastal farmland, the Netherlands has done more diking, draining, and filling of coastal wetlands in proportion to its size than any other country in the world. The

Dutch have increased their land area by more than one-third during their thousand-year struggle against the sea. In the United States, extensive flood control and channeling projects at the mouth of the Mississippi have cut the flow of sediments and fresh water into the Louisiana coastal wetlands; with their natural hydrology severely altered, they are now eroding away at a rate of 150 square kilometers per year.[38]

Coastal stabilization structures built to hold back the sea can hasten the loss of coastal habitat. Globally, the oceans have been rising 1 to 2 millimeters per year for the last 100 years, with a total rise of more than 100 meters since the last ice age (due to thermal expansion during this warming period). Retention walls erected to protect coastal property cut off wetlands from natural flushing, and halt the natural retreat of beaches. Beaches typically are eroded away within 50 years, leading to the eventual collapse of the retention wall. Breakwaters and jetties built out into the surf to protect harbors, channels and local beaches can alter coastal currents, depleting up-current habitat of the normal flow of sediments.[39]

Dams eliminate spawning habitat for species such as salmon, that spend part of their lives in the ocean and part in fresh water. In the southern part of the former Soviet Union (those countries surrounding the Black, Azov, Caspian, and Aral seas), water diversions for agriculture have eliminated 90 to 98 percent of the sturgeon, salmon, and other commercially valuable species that migrate in from the major rivers and estuaries. Overall, the share of runoff impounded by dams has been estimated at 20 percent in both North America and Africa, 15 percent in Europe, 14 percent in Asia, 6 percent in South America, and 4 percent in Oceania.[40]

Though less extensively than in coastal areas, pollution and habitat degradation also reach into the open ocean and deep sea. Researchers from Rutgers University, for example, found that a portion of the sewage sludge dumped off the coast of New Jersey reached the seabed 2,500 meters below and effectively doubled the deepwater food supply in that spot. Regulators had expected the 8 to 9 million wet tons of municipal wastes to disperse without a trace while sinking.[41]

An estimated 80 to 90 percent of the material dumped at sea comes from coastal dredging. At least 10 percent of it is contaminated with toxic materials from cities, industry, and shipping. DDT, PCBs and other persistent synthetic chemicals disperse into the oceans from coastal waters and the atmosphere, and garbage and oil slicks line the world's major shipping lanes. Countries have also used the deep ocean to dispose of military wastes and nuclear powered submarines. Although the dumping of nuclear and other highly toxic wastes at sea is prohibited, governments continue to consider the deep ocean for the disposal of hazardous wastes.[42]

As a result of flood control and channeling projects, Louisiana's coastal wetlands are eroding at a rate of 150 square kilometers per year.

Because of a lack ecological studies of the open oceans, the implications of this pollution are unknown. But there is some reason to believe these contaminants may have an effect disproportionate to their concentrations. Chemical pollutants tend to concentrate in the surface waters, which are also where larvae, eggs, and microorganisms concentrate. Heavy metals can be 10 to 100 times more concentrated near the surface than in the waters below, and pesticide residues can be *millions* of times stronger. These chemicals also tend to work their way up through the food chain and accumulate in the fat of marine mammals and other top predators.[43]

Even low levels of toxins may be too much for many open-ocean organisms. Because mid-ocean water has been historically so pure, its indigenous organisms are not adapted to changes in water chemistry like those now common along the coasts, and may be more sensitive to contaminants. Trace contaminants on ordinary laboratory glassware will kill the open ocean snail *pterapoda*, which takes up carbon dioxide to make its shell and then drops to the seabed when it dies.[44]

Direct destruction of deep sea habitat is uncommon, but it could become extensive if companies begin to mine the sea floor for minerals or use it as a disposal site for dangerous radioactive and toxic wastes. The seabed is scattered with nodules of manganese, nickel, zinc, and other valuable minerals that could be collected with large dredges. The technique is not yet economically feasible, however, and may not be for decades to come.

Among the future threats on the foreseeable horizon, global atmospheric changes loom large but uncertain. With the stratospheric ozone layer thinning due to the release of chlorofluorocarbons and other ozone-depleting chemicals into the atmosphere, greater quantities of the sun's tissue-damaging ultraviolet light are reaching the oceans. The increase is already reducing the productivity of phytoplankton in the Southern Ocean, where the South Pole stratospheric ozone layer thins by up to 50 percent with onset of the southern-hemispheric spring (September to December). Discovered in the 1980s, this "hole" in the protective ozone shield coincides with the longer days that trigger extensive phytoplankton blooms. University of California researchers found that the increased levels of ultraviolet light caused a minimum 6- to 12-percent reduction in phytoplankton productivity in areas under the hole, thereby reducing the supply of food in the Antarctic food chain and slowing the biological pump. Other marine life, such as larvae in the surface waters and corals, may also be suffering from the increased levels of ultraviolet light, and the damage could multiply as ozone depletion progresses.[45]

Even though the production and release of ozone-depleting chemicals is declining, the stratospheric ozone layer is expected to continue thinning into the next century due to the residual effects of the chemicals already in the atmosphere. As these dissipate, and if countries continue to reduce the production of ozone-depleters, the level of ultraviolet light should drop to safer levels, averting a potential ecological disaster. If, however, ozone depletion were to continue progressing for any reason, it would directly threaten the foundation of the marine food web and the biological pump.

The future effects of global warming on the oceans are even less certain. The buildup of carbon dioxide and other greenhouse gases in the atmosphere is expected to increase global temperatures and alter other climatic phenomena such as patterns of winds, rain, and severe storms. Rapid warming could disrupt temperature-sensitive ecosystems such as coral reefs, which have already suffered extensive die-offs of corals associated with higher water temperatures. Sea level rise would accelerate with global warming, and could inundate coastal habitats. Although a rise in water levels would not necessarily be detrimental to coastal ecosystems, the potentially disastrous effects on coastal cities and communities would likely result in attempts to hold back the sea with dikes and dams, in which case coastal habitat would be squeezed out. Because polar temperatures are likely to increase more than equatorial ones, the temperature difference that drives these currents would diminish, potentially altering oceanic currents. Scientists suspect that when Europe suffered the so-called Little Ice Age in the 1500s, it was due to a weakening in the Gulf Stream. Such changes could massively displace temperature- and nutrient-sensitive coastal habitats such as coral reefs, and alter the biological pump.[46]

Increased levels of ultraviolet light caused a 6 to 12 percent reduction in phytoplankton productivity under the ozone hole.

Devastating as they may be in theory, however, these global changes could—if they come on the heels of continued, unchecked degradation of coastal waters—be hardly noticeable in the aftermath of the damage already done. The die-off of corals in recent years, for instance, has been associated with high local temperatures, but scientists have been hard pressed to prove whether or not it is the heat that is stressing the corals, let alone whether global warming is the cause of the heat. Scientists meeting at a workshop on coral reefs in 1991 concluded that the die-offs could simply be the product of pollution, and that regardless of global warming, coral reefs are already severely threatened by pollution and direct destruction. Without the establishment of effective international, regional, and local policies to protect the coastal marine environment, future global changes may look like distant storm clouds seen from the midst of a hurricane.[47]

The Limits of the Sea

Fishers are the first to encounter the limits of the sea. Their increasing numbers, and the enormous capacity of the modern fishing fleet, have not only strained but, in many regions, severely exceeded the ability of marine life to reproduce and of the marine ecosystem to recover. While pollution and habitat destruction have harmed and weakened many marine organisms, the pursuit of food and other marine products has directly removed them in mass quantities. Trends in the world fish catch—not only the total but the changing composition—indicate that fishers are running up against global limits, while altering marine ecosystems in the process.

The marine species that succumb most readily to overexploitation are the slow-growing, long-lived, low-fertility animals such as mammals. The most dramatic example of a marine extinction was the Steller's sea cow (*Hydrodamalis gigas*), a mammal that lived in the North Pacific and weighed up to ten tons. In 1741, a Russian ship became stranded on Bering Island, where the sailors discovered the mammoth sea cows grazing the seagrasses offshore. The gentle behemoths were unafraid, making them easy prey for the hungry sailors. The men found the sea cow's meat and fat delectable, and lived off it until they reached safety and reported their good fortune. Subsequently, other ships sought out the region to stock up on food until the last Steller's sea cow was killed in 1768, only 27 years after the animal was discovered.[48]

Although the speed of this extinction was exceptional, hunters also have exterminated mammals such as the Caribbean monk seal and the Atlantic gray whale, and driven many more to the brink of extinction. Conservation agreements and laws now protect most of these endangered species, and some are on the rebound, but others are still threatened by hunting, fishing, habitat loss, and pollution.[49] (See Table 3.)

TABLE 3:
CHANGES IN MARINE MAMMAL POPULATIONS.

Species	Past Population (Mid-19th to mid-20th century)	Recent Population (Late 1980s to Present)
DECLINES		
Blue Whale	200,000	2,000
Right Whale	200,000	3,000
Bowhead Whale	120,000	6,000
Humpback Whale	125,000	10,000
Sei Whale	200,000	25,000
Fin Whale	470,000	110,000
Northern Sea Lion	154,000	66,000
Juan Fernandez Fur Seal	4,000,000	600
Hawaiian Monk Seal	2,500	1,000
RECOVERIES		
Pacific Gray Whale	10,000	21,000
Dugong	30,000	55,000
Walrus	50,000	280,000
Galapagos Fur Seal	Near-extinction	30,000
Antarctic Fur Seal	Near-extinction	1,530,000
EXTINCTIONS		
Atlantic Gray Whale	extinct, c.1730	
Steller's Sea Cow	extinct, c.1768	
Sea Mink	extinct, c.1880	
Caribbean Monk Seal	200	extinct, c.1952

Sources: See note 49.

Fishers and collectors are also jeopardizing coral reef species, such as turtles, sea cucumbers, mother of pearl, and other coveted exotic organisms, decimating whole populations of these relatively rare species to meet the demand for specialty products. Hunters have eliminated giant clams from reef after reef in Southeast Asia because the mollusc's meat is a high-priced delicacy in the region. Many of the fish and other marine life that live on coral reefs are particularly vulnerable to overfishing because, like mammals, they are long-lived and have low fertility.[50]

The proliferation of fishers, combined with the greatly increased capacity of their equipment, has now begun to put more fertile and populous species at risk as well. Sonar and aircraft enable fishers to locate schools of fish in the open ocean, and giant nets allow them to literally strain the sea of fish. The mouth of a recently designed Icelandic trawling net, for example, is large enough to simultaneously trap 12 Boeing 747 airplanes in piles of six. According to the activist group Greenpeace, even larger trawlers are under construction.[51]

Overfishing has precipitated declines in individual stocks throughout the world. The catch of four commonly eaten, average-value fish (Atlantic cod, Cape hake, haddock, and silver hake) fell from 5 million tons in 1970 to 2.6 million tons in 1989. Canada has placed a two-year moratorium on cod fishing off Newfoundland to try to stem the decline in fish stocks, and the European Community is restricting cod fishing as well. FAO concludes that depletion of various stocks has occurred in virtually all coastal states throughout the world.[52]

The fish catch from the oceans grew rapidly through the middle decades of this century, but has begun to falter. Starting from under 5 million tons in 1900, the documented annual catch rose to over 80 million tons in recent years. (See Figure 3.) Between 1950 and 1970, annual increases were 6 percent per year—three times the rate of human population growth during that era. Then, in the early 1970s, the Peruvian anchovy catch, the largest in the world, collapsed from 12 million to 2 million tons per year over the course of three years. This event, apparently due to the combined effects of overfishing and natural fluctuations, marked the beginning of a new era. For the next two decades, the marine catch grew by only 2.3 percent per year, and after peaking at 86 million tons in 1989, it fell by 7 percent over the next three years back to 80 million tons in 1992.[53]

Like the crash of the Peruvian anchovy catch before it, the recent three-year decline may mark a new era in marine fishing.

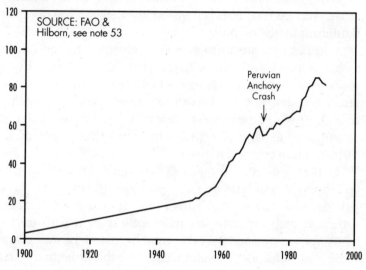

FIGURE 3:

World Marine Fish Catch, 1900–2000

Million tons

SOURCE: FAO & Hilborn, see note 53

Peruvian Anchovy Crash

Fishers have managed to keep the marine fish catch climbing in past decades by abandoning fished-out stocks and pursuing new species. These substitutions, however, are typically lower-value fish that were previously undesirable and unwanted because they were deemed too small, bony, poor-tasting, or otherwise not good for eating. Five species—Alaska pollack, Chilean jack mackerel, Japanese pilchard, South American pilchard, and the rebounding Peruvian anchovy—have made up most of the production increases in the 1980s. But Alaska pollack has only one-third the value of the Atlantic cod, an average-priced eating fish, and the other four have only a tenth the value of cod. Although these five species accounted for 29 percent of the world fish catch by weight in 1989, they made up only 6 percent of the total value.[54]

Besides having a low economic value, small shoaling species such as the anchovy and the pilchard make only a minimal contribution to human nutrition, since they are primarily used for animal feed, fertilizer, or other industrial products. About 30 percent of the world fish catch goes to these secondary uses. Small shoaling species also tend to fluctuate widely in numbers, as demonstrated by the 1970 crash of the Peruvian anchovy catch. And FAO scientists believe that these species will not yield significant increases in the future.[55]

Without new stocks to exploit, overfishing has become a global problem. FAO now estimates that all 17 of the world's major fishing areas have either reached or exceeded their natural limits, and that 9 of the areas are in serious decline. According to FAO, "there is little reason to believe that the global catch can continue to expand, except for increases that might occur through more effective management of stocks."[56]

In 1971, a study sponsored by FAO estimated that the marine environment could sustainably yield about 100 million tons of fish per year, 20 million tons more than the 1992 catch. Although such estimates are inherently fraught with uncertainty, the recent faltering of the world catch and the state of the world's major fishing grounds indicate that this projection could be close to the mark, though optimistic. Today, FAO scientists believe that the world catch is unlikely to reach and maintain the projected 100 million tons unless stocks are better managed. At best, future gains in the marine catch will not come as easily as in the past, if they come at all.[57]

Overfishing has broader implications for the marine environment, as well. One of the most pervasive problems is that fishers catch, kill and discard large quantities of unwanted species, known as "bycatch." The most infamous technique of fishing that results in a high rate of bycatch is high seas driftnetting. The data from observers for the U.S. National Oceanic and Atmospheric Administration indicates that in 1990, driftnetters ensnared some 42 million seabirds, marine mammals and other nontarget species in pursuit of tuna and squid. Tuna fishers in the eastern tropical Pacific Ocean have also achieved international notoriety because they have traditionally sought out and encircled dolphin herds with their purse-seine nets to catch the tuna schools that can be found swimming below. Purse-seine fishers killed more than 400,000 dolphins per year at the peak of this practice in the 1970s. Both of these practices, however, are in decline due to grassroots activism and international pressure.[58]

Other forms of net fishing today result in a greater amount of dead and discarded bycatch. Coastal trawlers, which drag nets along the seabed, catch large quantities of unwanted species. Shrimp trawlers probably have the highest rate of bycatch, bring in up to 90 percent or more "trash fish" with each haul in tropical waters. Worldwide, shrimp fishers are estimated to discard up to 15 million tons of unwanted fish per year, and other fishers are thought to discard another 5 million tons.[59]

At the other extreme of selectivity, but with equally decimating effect, there is the growing practice of "biomass fishing," in which fishers in some countries take all the fish they can catch with fine-mesh trawling equipment. Much of this clean-sweep catch goes to meet the growing demand for feed for fish farming. In the most entropic possible disregard for the values of biological diversity, hundreds of interdependent species are ground up into a mash to feed a few monocultured fish.[60]

FAO now estimates that all 17 of the world's major fishing areas have either reached or exceeded their natural limits.

As fishers remove an ever greater proportion of the biomass from the marine environment, entire ecosystems begin to suffer. In the Shetland Islands, Arctic terns, puffins, and other nesting birds failed to breed in the mid and late 1980s, apparently due to overfishing of the sand eel, a small shoaling fish caught for fish meal and oil. The birds normally fed young sand eels to their chicks, but the fish's population declined with the commercial catch, which peaked at 56,000 tons in 1982 and then slid to 4,800 tons in 1988. In a similar collapse, off the coast of Peru, guano birds abandoned their young when the Peruvian anchovy fishery collapsed. In the North Pacific, Steller's sea lion, dolphin, and bird populations apparently have declined in recent years due to heavy fishing of Alaskan pollack. And in Kenya, researchers found that heavy fishing of triggerfish on coral reefs allowed the proliferation of rock-boring sea urchins that were endangering the entire ecosystem.[61]

The heavily fished North Sea shows signs of extensive stress. North Sea trawlers alter the fish populations by hauling out the larger adult fish and allowing only juveniles and smaller species to survive. Scientists believe that cod and haddock populations will soon have too few adults to maintain their numbers. The trawlers discard 2 to 4 kilograms of fish killed in their nets for every kilogram of desired fish caught. Porpoises and dolphins, too, are apparently disappearing not only because of pollution and drowning in fishers' nets, but also because of the depletion of the fish they eat.[62]

In the Dutch region of the North Sea, researchers have found that every square meter of the seabed is disturbed at least once a year by trawlers dragging nylon nets held open by beams and weighed down by chains. In the heavily trafficked areas, trawlers make an average of seven passes per year with these nets that weigh up to 5 tons each. The nets and chains dig into the sea bed and kill sea urchins, starfish, worms, crustaceans, and shellfish, severely damaging the ecosystem.[63]

Overfishing of commercially valuable herring and mackerel in the North Sea in recent decades apparently altered the ecological balance in favor of a less-valuable species of fish called gadoids. Fishers increased the likelihood that gadoids will survive to adulthood by removing mass quantities of herring and mackerel, which normally prey on gadoid larvae. Uncontrolled by their natural predators, the gadoids reach adult size in unnatural numbers. The adult gadoids then eat herring and juvenile mackerel, further decreasing these commercial fish stocks. Bluefin tuna, which also prey on herring and mackerel, have in turn declined.[64]

Overfishing has social implications, as well, particularly for people in the fishing industry itself, who inevitably suffer when the fish catch begins to slump. Worldwide, this industry directly employs some 200 million people, many of whom now find their jobs threatened. In Canada alone, between 30,000 and 50,000 people were put out of work when the country had to shut down its cod fishery to allow stocks to recover. In France, fishers fearing for their livelihoods have protested violently against the import of low-priced fish from Russia and other non-European Community countries. Peaceful demonstrations have turned violent when protestors set off small explosives and broke windows, and fishers have fought street battles with police all along the French coast. In the town of Rungis, protestors battled police for three hours, flinging fish, overturning market stands, and causing $4.5 million in damage. Fishers have also come into direct conflict with each other over fishing stocks. In Indonesia, small-scale fishers have attacked and burned shrimp-trawling vessels that encroach on their fishing grounds. Coast guard officials entrusted with protecting the coastal waters from illegal trawlers have reportedly trawled with nets from their own boats and taken kickbacks to allow foreign vessels to ply the Indonesian waters.[65]

Local fishers who use small boats and traditional techniques inevitably suffer from depleted stocks.

With their limited political power and equipment, local fishers who use small boats and traditional techniques inevitably suffer from depleted stocks. In the Indian state of Kerala, for example, the government promoted and subsidized commercial fishing for export, which put poor fishers who could not afford commercial-scale boats and equipment at a disadvantage. The subsidized, mass-production techniques led to overfishing of the coastal waters, further undermining the livelihood of the traditional fishers. And the livelihood of small-scale fishers is threatened by foreign fleets, as well as by their own countries' shortsighted subsidies. Off the coast of Sierra Leone in West Africa, uncontrolled fishing by foreign fleets led to a decline in the catch of traditional fishers, who supply 75 percent of the country's own consumption of animal protein. The foreign fleets primarily export their catch, so the negative impact of the commercial incursion then spreads beyond the fishers' families to the population at large.[66]

Increased international demand and rising prices have thus put fishers and consumers in developing countries in a tight bind. Third World countries are exporting an increasing percentage of their fish catch in order to gain the foreign exchange needed to pay off pressing foreign debts. Exports of ocean products from developing countries have increased twice as fast as those from the industrial countries, and imports into developed countries now stand at nearly *seven* times those into developing countries. On average, people in the industrial world eat three times as much fish as their Third-World counterparts, despite the higher dependence in developing countries on this source of animal protein.[67]

Increasing poverty, in turn, drives the fishing problem into an even more vicious circle. As fish become more scarce, more fishers turn to destructive practices such as biomass fishing, and some even resort to fishing with poisons or dynamite. In a Southeast Asian practice known as *muro-ami,* children are forced to swim through the water pounding coral reefs with rocks tied to brightly colored streamers to scare the fish towards waiting nets. Besides damaging the corals and depleting the reef, muro-ami endangers the lives of the children, some of whom are killed by needlefish, sharks, barracuda, poisonous sea snakes and disease. In the Philippines, one corporation has been responsible for running 40 muro-ami ships that carry up to 300 boys and collectively destroy as much as a square kilometer of reef per day. The children are reportedly taken from the poor barrios of the big cities. This is yet another consequence of the spiraling mechanism by which poverty and the degrading of the oceans become mutually aggravating; as food becomes scarcer inland, more people migrate to the coasts to take up fishing, the "employer of last resort," because they have open access to the water. In response to increased competition and declining natural stocks, some coastal fishers have turned to fish farming, which, as noted earlier, puts its own pressures on ocean ecology.[68]

Beyond pointing to the increasingly detrimental effects both on the oceans and on the people who rely on them, the faltering catch of marine life is an indicator of the declining health of the marine ecosystem. As pollution, habitat destruction, and overfishing progress, they limit the oceans' ability to help meet the global demand for food. The measure of coastal degradation is often the decline of useable stocks, such as that of the Chesapeake Bay oysters. Indeed, the phrase "there are always more fish in the sea" begins to sound rather quaintly and sadly dated, now that we are seeing just how finite the oceans' biological systems are. We have not only unwittingly run into the limits of the sea through fishing, but we have even started to reduce those limits by degrading the oceans.

Governing the Sea

Historically, oceans law has focused on the freedom to use the seas for economic and military purposes. In his 1608 landmark treatise *Mare Liberum*, Dutch legal scholar Hugo Grotius defined a country's territorial sea as the distance a cannon ball could be shot to defend the waters, which was later commonly accepted as 3 nautical miles (5.6 kilometers). Beyond that range, the ocean was open to all. Ships could do as they pleased, and even fishing was unregulated because fish stocks were held to be practically limitless. Within the 3 mile limit, ships were bound by the laws of the coastal country.[69]

Although more restrictive today, oceans law has held to Grotius's basic concept of an open sea ringed by nationally controlled coastal zones. International treaties and customary law (such as *Mare Liberum*) govern activities on the high seas, define the scope of national jurisdiction over coastal areas, and establish some common standards and procedures for coordinating management and resolving conflicts between countries.

In addressing high-profile environmental issues, oceans law has advanced steadily in recent decades. International negotiators have worked out agreements on oil spills, ocean dumping, and whaling and sealing. Some types of marine pollution have abated, as has the exploitation of some marine mammals. But the major treaties have largely overlooked the less charismatic but more pervasive issues of land-based sources of pollution, habitat destruction, and overfishing, even in terms of setting standards. Without global agreements to address these critical issues, the broader goal of protecting Earth's greatest commons will be difficult, if not impossible, to achieve. International law will not guarantee protection, but it will provide a basis for responsible and effective management by individual nations.

Mare Liberum has evolved into what is now known as the Law of the Sea, a United Nations-mediated treaty on the management of the oceans. Starting with the first set of negotiations in 1958, international delegates have convened three times to update and codify what is essentially the constitution of the oceans. The agreements themselves have only limited environmental provisions, but they do define the context within which local and regional conservation occurs. In the third set of negotiations, which stretched from 1973 to 1982, the delegates agreed to expand the territorial sea from 3 to 12 nautical miles, and to create a 200 nautical mile coastal area—called the Exclusive Economic Zone (EEZ)—within which the coastal country has exclusive rights to the natural resources. By 1976, 60 countries had claimed EEZs of their own, and although the third Law of the Sea has so far fallen short of ratification, the concept has become an accepted part of customary oceans law.[70]

EEZs effectively take the most valuable portion of the oceans out of the realm of global commons and place it within the jurisdiction of coastal states (see Map). In response to this change in international law, coastal countries, particularly in the Third World, have taken greater control over their adjacent waters. Unfortunately, most coastal countries have been more attentive to increasing short-term revenues than to conserving long-term assets, and have tended to overexploit their fish stocks. The Law of the Sea draws a rather fine distinction in this respect, urging coastal nations to avoid overexploitation, while at the same time calling on them to allow foreign fleets to fish in their waters if fish stocks are not fully exploited domestically. In the face of the growing number of empty-hulled vessels scouring the globe for still-productive fishing grounds, the language about conservation may be little more than exhortation.[71]

The Law of the Sea does contain a section concerned expressly with protecting the marine environment. For the most part, its provisions assign responsibility for environmental protection at both the national and international level, with generally vague and unenforceable language. It does, however, require countries to adopt, implement, and enforce the rules and standards of other global treaties, such as those on oil spills and ocean dumping. By effectively making existing agreements the minimum international standard, the Law of the Sea would—if ratified—extend their coverage. For example, only 39 countries have so far ratified the international agreement that restricts dumping sewage from ships, but if the Law of the Sea is ratified, all of the parties to it (at least 60 countries) would have to abide by this annex to the 1973/1978 treaty on pollution from ships (MARPOL).[72]

The Law of the Sea itself is not yet in force primarily because of opposition from the United States to the treaty's seabed mining provisions. The negotiated text established an International Seabed Authority to regulate and collect royalties from companies that collect the minerals on the deep ocean floor. The Reagan administration, which was just entering office as the negotiations were ending in 1981, opposed the international regulation and reversed the U.S. position on the final treaty. Without the political and financial support of the United States, other industrial nations have been reluctant to commit to the Law of the Sea. Despite the fact that over 120 countries indicated support for the Law of the Sea in 1983, the number that have actually ratified the text still remains—over a decade later— three short of the 60 needed to bring it into force.[73]

Recent negotiations on the seabed mining provisions involving the United States may break the deadlock, leading to full acceptance of the third Law of the Sea in the near future. While this updated version of the constitution of the oceans would strengthen international marine protection, it would still rely on issue-specific treaties such as MARPOL; thus the Law of the Sea still would fail to effectively address the most fundamental causes of degradation. Although a fourth round of Law of the Sea negotiations could address the outstanding issues, countries appear reluctant to reopen the general debate at this time. More likely, advances in marine protection will come from issue-specific international negotiations.[74]

Among all the human activities affecting the oceans, shipping has attracted the greatest amount of global attention and regulation. The International Maritime Organization (IMO) was established three decades ago to regulate shipping internationally. Over the years, various disasters at sea have raised cleanup and liability issues that have given rise to a series of international treaties covering pollution and dumping from ships and the transport of hazardous materials. Under these IMO-administered agreements, signatory countries have adopted international standards and enforced them under their domestic laws with some success. Between 1981 and 1989, oil pollution from ships dropped by 60 percent, according to a study conducted by the U.S. National Academy of Sciences. Under the London Dumping Convention of 1972, signatory countries banned ocean dumping of highly toxic pollutants and high-level radioactive waste, and since 1983 they have observed a moratorium on dumping low-level radioactive wastes. The 70 member countries of the London Dumping Convention are in the process of making the moratorium into a permanent ban.[75]

Among the issues yet to be confronted, the one most likely to come under an international agreement in the foreseeable future is the proliferating introduction of exotic species. The usually inadvertent transport of marine life, especially in ballast water, now affects all the coastal countries of the world. The issue is becoming more visible with the increasing outbreaks of toxic algal blooms (red tides) and associated poisonings and fishery closures. The IMO, with particular prodding from Australia, has ratified voluntary guidelines on ballast water and is considering binding regulations.[76]

In agreements covering shipping, the key issues include participation, implementation, and enforcement. No agreement has satisfied every country, though the basic marine pollution agreement (MARPOL)—with 70 signatory countries, representing 90 percent of the world merchant fleet—has high acceptance. Fewer countries have agreed to MARPOL's special provisions, such as the restrictions on dumping ship sewage. Under current international law, a ship on the open ocean cannot be held to a treaty's provisions unless its flag country is a participant.[77]

Signing an agreement can be a largely empty gesture if a country does not take steps to implement the provisions. For instance, if a nation has agreed to the MARPOL provisions that prohibit dumping plastics and restrict dumping other ship waste at sea, it is supposed to install special port-side waste collection facilities so that ships can dispose of their waste without importing infectious diseases and noxious pests. If a port doesn't have these facilities, ships are supposed to hold their wastes until they reach one that does. But many ships, rather than undergo this inconvenience, are incinerating their wastes and dumping the ash at sea, releasing the toxins into the marine environment. Some countries also use loopholes in the treaties to allow practices that are outside the spirit of the agreement, such as dumping toxic wastes.[78]

Between 1981 and 1989, oil pollution from ships dropped by 60 percent.

Enforcement is another matter. Illegal discharge of wastes is believed to be a global problem that has killed tens of thousands of birds and harmed other marine life. These treaties only work if individual countries establish laws that codify the international standards domestically and then implement systems to detect and punish people who break the laws. Because action on the oceans is hard to monitor, record keeping is helpful to enforcement officials. For example, the United States and Norway decided to require log entries for the disposal of ship wastes, even though MARPOL did not.[79]

In contrast with shipping, fishing agreements are still in the formative stage. Countries cooperate on gathering and sharing information, but have been reluctant to enter into binding international agreements. However, recent international conflicts over dwindling fish stocks have drawn scores of countries to the bargaining table. In July, 1993, 150 diplomats convened in the U.N.'s New York City headquarters to follow up on the fishery provisions of Agenda 21, the core agreement resulting from the 1992 Earth Summit. The talks focused on fish that swim across lines of national jurisdictions, bringing countries into direct conflict. The July meeting resulted in a preliminary text for further negotiations in 1994. Two camps have formed—one around the interests of countries with major fishing grounds who want a binding international treaty, and one around those with long-range fishing fleets, who want only a guideline. The talks, however, will not address overfishing of undisputed coastal waters.[80]

Agreements to halt the decimation of marine mammals have been more successful than their fishing counterparts. The first international treaty on the take of marine life was the 1911 Convention for the Preservation and Protection of Fur Seals, which was negotiated in the face of plummeting seal populations due to uncontrolled hunting. The four signatory countries (Russia, Japan, the United States, and Great Britain on behalf of Canada) agreed to allow hunting of the North Pacific fur seal only on specific breeding islands, and the countries that gave up the right to hunting seals at sea received compensation. The number of seals soared from 125,000 in 1911 to 2,300,000 in 1941.[81]

The International Whaling Commission (IWC), established in 1947 by whaling nations to coordinate their efforts, did not begin to orient its efforts toward conservation until the 1970s, when non-whaling nations started joining the commission. In 1985, having achieved a majority of conservation-oriented members, the IWC enacted a moratorium on whaling. Iceland withdrew from the Commission in protest, and Japan has continued to kill approximately 300 minke whales per year for "scientific" purposes—many of which end up in high-price restaurants and shops. At the 1993 meeting of IWC, a majority of the member countries voted to uphold the whaling ban. That decision drew bitter protests from Norwegian and Japanese delegates, who argued that IWC research shows that minke whales, with a population of 87,000 in Barents Sea off Norway and 760,000 around Antarctica, can be sustainably harvested. While that claim has not been definitively refuted, the IWC does not have detailed information on minke reproduction, nor has it established a working plan for enforcing whaling quotas. Following the IWC meeting, Norway announced that it would resume whaling, and in the 1993 season its whalers killed 157 minke whales.[82]

Even so, the marine mammal treaties, which have brought voluntary compliance by many countries and have introduced at least some stability to previously threatened populations, stand in notable contrast to the lack of any substantive treaty for the protection of coastal waters. Pollution from land-based sources, coastal habitat destruction, and overfishing of coastal waters continue to be the greatest threats to the marine environment. Yet, through the EEZ, international law has placed the most biologically vulnerable and economically valuable parts of the oceans—the coastal waters—outside of its realm without any defined or enforceable responsibilities to protect these waters from degradation. Coastal nations are in the best position to manage this portion of the global commons, but currently they are not accountable to the international community for their actions.

In Agenda 21, the delegates to the Earth Summit acknowledged the growing crisis in coastal areas, but once again the international community was reluctant to call for specific global agreements or standards that would cross the traditional line of national sovereignty over coastal waters. The Earth Summit, however, will result in international meetings and conferences to address pollution from land-based sources and coastal zone management, which could in the future lead to global agreements and standards. The U.N. Environment Programme (UNEP), for instance, is supposed to convene an intergovernmental meeting on the protection of the marine environment from land-based activities. One possibility would be to upgrade UNEP's 1985 Montreal Guidelines on Land-Based Pollution, which is currently just a checklist for interested countries. Coastal habitat protection fell lower on the international agenda, but the World Coast Conference, held in The Hague in November 1993, could likewise lead to global standards on habitat protection.[83]

Although this follow-up on Agenda 21 is promising, for it to come to any substantive ends, countries will have to relinquish some of their traditional notions of sovereignty over coastal waters. The health of the oceans depends on the actions of all countries. Global standards would prevent one country from nullifying the environmental gains made by another.

Shoring up the Sea

Without far more serious attention by governments, industry, and communities to the biological limits of the oceans, marine and coastal environments will continue to deteriorate, eroding land-based as well as sea-based economies, and threatening the ecological keel of the biosphere. The conundrum of ocean protection is that the marine environment is one of the earth's great commons, but its most productive zones are under national jurisdictions. Given the direct influence of coastal countries on the oceans, along with the weaknesses of current international law, it will be largely up to the individual nations and local communities to take the specific actions necessary to turn the tide of marine degradation.

The three areas of highest priority for more protective management are fishing, coastal development, and inland sources of pollution. These are the largest causes of degradation, and represent the greatest opportunities for reversal.

The first step is to halt the depletion of fish stocks, in part by re-establishing basic tenets of local fisheries management and conservation that were once widely observed in traditional Pacific Island and coastal cultures but have been disappearing under the weight of the consumer culture, centralized governments, and aggressive competition from foreign fleets.[84]

Many of the traditional tenets of fishery management are still applicable and, with the support of national governments, could provide workable means of restoring vitality to local fisheries. Much of the biological hemorrhage can be stemmed by placing limits or bans on blatantly harmful fishing practices such as biomass fishing and other methods with high levels of bycatch. For example, a fisheries researcher from the Senegal Agricultural Research Institute has proposed that trawlers could increase their long-term catch by using nets with larger mesh, which would prevent stocks from declining by allowing the smaller fish to escape and reproduce.[85]

Likewise, limitations on fishing seasons, size of catch, access to fishing grounds, and the boundaries within which fishing is permitted, can all serve to restrict the catch. New Zealand has pioneered the use of no-fishing zones among industrial countries. Within these zones, fish are allowed to mature and reproduce unmolested, leading to increased overall stocks. Furthermore, no-fishing zones leave the local habitat intact.[86]

Restrictions on commercial fishing not only directly bolster stocks, but can benefit traditional fishers, thereby reducing the pressure on them to resort to destructive practices such as bio-mass fishing. In Sierra Leone, for instance, traditional fishers found their catch declining as that of visiting commercial fish-ers from Europe increased. Because commercial fishers export, while the traditional fishers feed local people, it behooved the government to protect the traditional fishers' stocks. Sierra Leone established a five-mile fishing zone along the coast where only traditional fishers can fish, and sought to limit overfishing by commercial fishers outside that area. Because the country lacked the resources to patrol the commercial fishing waters, it established an experimental self-policing policy under which one foreign-based company issued the fishing licenses and enforced fishing regulations. Under this experiment, the num-ber of foreign boats fell from around 170 to 50, and poaching fell off due to constant patrols.[87]

To limit traditional fishing requires a similar form of self-policing with government support. The best examples parallel traditional community-based management. In the Philippines, the government grants local communities 25-year contracts to manage their sections of the coast. With this authority, sever-al communities have restored hundreds of hectares of man-groves, established no-fishing zones, and limited fishing, with resulting increases in the sustainable fish catch.[88]

The broader problem that decision-makers need to confront is the proverbial "too many fishers chasing too few fish." The undeniable fact is that national fishing fleets have grown too big for existing stocks. FAO conservatively estimates that globally, annual expenditures on fishing amount to $124 billion, in order to catch just $70 billion worth of fish. Governments apparent-ly make up most of the $54 billion difference with low interest loans, access fees for foreign fishing grounds, and direct subsidies for boats and operations. These government subsidies keep more people fishing than the oceans can support.[89]

Open access to fishing grounds contributes to the bloated size of fishing fleets. Without restrictions on access, people continue to take up fishing well after the maximum sustainable catch has been surpassed in their areas. Once invested, fishers will only pull out of an area if they can find new fishing grounds where they can use their equipment; otherwise they will stick with the overfished grounds until forced out of business. Government subsidies exacerbate this problem, creating a self-perpetuating cycle that leads to the collapse of the fish stocks.

Rather than carrying the industry as a net budgetary burden, countries could collect rents for the use of fishing grounds as a part of a larger management strategy to limit access. As in the management of grazing, logging or mining on public lands, fees are essential to limiting exploitation and compensating the public for the use of commonly held resources. In Australia, for example, rents for the use of fishing grounds have ranged from 11 to 60 percent of the gross value of the catch, with a weighted average of 30 percent. Such rents could be adjusted according to the status of the fish stocks, with fees increasing as the stocks become more depleted. They would also serve to streamline the world fishing fleet.[90]

Worldwide, the fiscal and economic benefits of improved management would be on the order of tens of billions of dollars per year. Governments could potentially save some $54 billion per year by eliminating subsidies, and earn another $25 billion per year in rents, with a net budgetary benefit of more than the current *gross* value of the entire marine catch. Meanwhile, if stocks are allowed to recover, FAO estimates that fishers could increase their annual catch by as much as 20 million tons, worth about $16 billion at today's prices. Although this theoretical exercise does not take into account the broader adjustments that societies will have to undergo to redirect former fishers into other occupations, it conveys the magnitude of economic mismanagement that has contributed to the ecological mismanagement of the oceans.[91]

Besides limiting overfishing, future management needs to take into account the broader effects of fishing on the marine environment. An apparently sustainable yield of one species can still harm other species or the entire ecosystem. In an attempt to avoid this problem, the Commission for the Conservation of Antarctic Marine Living Resources (CCAMLR), which regulates the removal of marine life in the Southern Ocean (except that of whales and seals which are covered by other treaties), established an ecosystem approach to the management of the Antarctic fishery. In 1991, the commission set a limit on the catch of krill, the small zooplankton that form a vital link in the Antarctic food chain.

Some environmentalists have questioned the methodology by which the limit (1.5 million tons per year in the southern Atlantic) was established. Indeed, establishing reasonable quotas may prove difficult, whether for krill, cod or any other marine life. Researchers from the University of Washington and the University of British Columbia say that the notion of "sustainable yield" is an elusive goal because natural fluctuations in fish stocks

Governments could save some $54 billion per year by eliminating subsidies.

and illegal fishing are part of the system but would be hard to account for. Nonetheless, the CCAMLR limit sets an important precedent, by approaching the problem of depletion proactively—implementing a solution before the problem has become a crisis.[92]

On land, where the main causes of ocean depredation are pollution and habitat destruction, the highest priority of oceans management is to control coastal development. A first step would be to eliminate subsidies such as government-sponsored insurance and funding for ocean-altering roads, dikes, and dams. The Netherlands, for instance, spends $400 million per year to pump water and repair inland dikes, despite the fact that the Dutch are producing more food than they can use or sell abroad, burdening the country with high payments to farmers to cover their excess production. To save money and begin rehabilitating the coastal ecosystem, the government has made plans to return 150,000 hectares of farmland (15 percent of the total converted area) to the sea over the next 25 years. Although the Dutch plan to continue diking and developing the coastal zone, this reversal reflects the country's growing awareness of the long-range importance of managing the coasts for ecological, as well as economic, purposes.[93]

Natural buffer zones can protect coastal habitat from nearby development. Natural wetlands, for instance, trap toxins, pathogens and excess nutrients and sediments as they move seaward, while also protecting coastal communities from storms and sea surges. Governments may eventually need to consider restricting or even prohibiting further coastal development altogether, in light of the predicted sea level rise of 0.6 meters over the next 100 years and the increased likelihood of stronger storms from sea.[94]

Where rural communities use coastal habitat, management efforts can moderate their effect on the natural environment. Ecuador, for instance, which in the past 23 years has lost 80,000 hectares of mangrove forests and salt flats to shrimp ponds, has begun a national program for the management of its coastal resources. The program stemmed from a U.S. Agency for International Development pilot project to slow the rapid degradation of Ecuador's coastal resources while still allowing local communities to benefit from them. For example, since the shrimp industry is a sizable portion of Ecuador's exports and economy (nearly 80,000 metric tons of shrimp, worth almost $500 million in 1991), the project emphasized training to help Ecuadorian shrimp farmers protect the coastal environment while maintaining their livelihoods.[95]

A similar incentive—to give long-term protection to an important sector of the economy—comes from coastal tourism, which draws about half of all national and international travelers. This incentive has prompted nations from Southeast Asia to Europe to clean up their coastlines and invest in marine protection. In Thailand's Surat Thani Province on the Gulf of Thailand, the coral reefs in Ban Don Bay attracted an increasing number of tourists in the 1980s, leading the provincial government to crack down on damaging fishing practices and prohibit the destruction of reefs for the construction of hotels.

Local governments and organizations are also implementing a coral management plan to control excessively invasive tourism, pollution, and overfishing, and to raise public awareness.[96]

Only a tiny proportion of the coastal environment is—or can be—set aside for special protection. But marine parks, sanctuaries, and other protected areas can single out highly vulnerable ecosystems. Australia, for instance, made the entire 350,000 square kilometers of the Great Barrier Reef into a park in 1975, and placed it under a single park authority. But rather than closing the reef to all but non-intrusive tourism and science, the park authority is charged with managing the reef for multiple uses. Some areas are completely off-limits to everyone except research scientists, while others are open to tourists, and still others are open to commercial fishing and even to the collection of corals.[97]

The theory behind the Great Barrier Reef Park's "integrated coastal management" system is that there is no way the entire marine environment could be entirely closed to people. Nor, say its administrators, would it work if some parts were closed off as marine sanctuaries while other areas that affect them were left to uncontrolled use. The Australian system hopes to insure the long term viability of the entire ecosystem by coordinating and managing its use. The largest shortcoming of the park's management is pollution from inland sources; the park authority can regulate the release of pollutants directly into the park, but it has no control over the pollution flowing from inland.[98]

Efforts to clean up marine pollution will more likely succeed if they are combined with overarching efforts to improve the quality of drinking water, food, and air.

Thus, the third major priority of oceans management is to reduce the flow of pollution from land. Of all the pollutants entering the oceans worldwide, 33 percent come via air emissions from land-based sources, and 44 percent via rivers and streams. These diffuse sources pose the stiffest of all ocean- protection challenges, but because they also contribute to the deterioration of the immediate human environment, we have strong motivation to control them. Efforts to clean up these sources of pollution will more likely succeed if—instead of being treated as separate marine-pollution projects—they are combined with overarching efforts to improve the quality and safety of drinking water, food, and air.[99]

Among the waterborne pollutants reaching the oceans, sewage is a matter of primary concern not only for the sake of the marine environment, but also for human health. Some 1.7 billion people in the developing world do not have sanitary ways to dispose of their sewage. Successful treatment can vary from sanitary pit latrines to advanced sewage treatment plants. Water recycling efforts, such as those pioneered by Israel, can further reduce the input of excess nutrients into the aquatic environment, while conserving scarce water supplies.[100]

Clean-water legislation, while not normally conceived as a response to ocean degradation, is helpful in mitigating it. In industrial countries such as Japan, Germany and the United States, manufacturers have reduced the output of pollutants in response to these laws. In the United States, farmers have reduced the erosion of soil, which carries fertilizers and pesticides, in response to farm legislation. These efforts to control water pollution help to protect the health of the rivers that pass through farmland, the people who draw drinking water from them downstream, and the coastal waters into which they flow. Similar benefits accrue from clean-air and pesticides laws.[101]

For these sorts of pan-regional pollution control efforts to succeed, they need broader coordination. But it is not enough for coastal waters to be protected from pollution only as an incidental benefit, since coastal ecosystems have unique needs of their own. Among the few efforts that have been made specifically to protect the marine environment from pollution, one of the most advanced programs is that which was enacted for the Chesapeake Bay, the largest bay estuary in the United States. The estuary is fed by over 150 tributary rivers and streams coming from an area the size of Cambodia spread over six states and the District of Columbia. Under the Chesapeake Bay Agreement of

1987, the District of Columbia and the states of Virginia, Maryland, and Pennsylvania agreed to reduce nutrients by 40 percent by the year 2000, control the discharge of toxins, and increase wetland area.[102]

Although the agreement itself is an important landmark, the signatories have had mixed success in carrying through. On one hand, seagrass area has increased by 57 percent, the Potomac River (one of the main tributaries) is much cleaner, and phosphorus levels are down by 20 percent. On the other, runoff from agriculture has increased, the population in the region continues to grow rapidly, development adjacent to the bay coastline continues, and, as a result, the load of nitrogen nutrients entering the bay is still increasing.[103]

The limited success of the Chesapeake Bay project demonstrates the difficulty of implementing such programs even in a single country. In many other instances, cooperation between neighboring countries is necessary, creating an even greater challenge. Such alliances become more difficult when some of the participating countries are economically disadvantaged. Thus, in the Mediterranean, the diversity of economic, political, and ethnic backgrounds made the initial formation of a Mediterranean Action Plan an historic achievement. The Mediterranean Regional Sea Programme has struggled in its efforts to set pollution standards and time tables for meeting them, but is still notable for having brought together old enemies such as Syria, Israel and Lebanon, and Greece and Turkey for the sake of their common sea. It also helped to launch the U.N. Environment Programme (UNEP)'s Regional Seas Programmes, ten of which have been organized around the world, with more than 120 participating countries. The programs have focused conservation efforts, public debate, and scientific research on the problems of land-based sources of marine pollution, as well as on species and habitat protection, and emergency spill and pollution plans.[104]

Under the UNEP programs, each region tailors its priorities to specific regional problems. In West and Central Africa, program goals include adequate water supplies, prevention of coastal erosion, and reuse of wastewater for agriculture. In the South

Pacific, island nations are negotiating controls on ocean dumping, a ban on radioactive waste dumping and storage, and an end to nuclear weapons testing in the area. In the Kuwait region of the Persian Gulf and the Gulf of Oman, eight regional partners are working to improve sewage treatment, protect fisheries resources, and control offshore drilling and hazardous waste transport. To date, the Kuwait region has been the only Regional Seas program to pass pollution regulations specifically for gas and oil rig platforms harbored at sea.[105]

Despite these substantive successes, the Regional Seas Programmes have foundered in recent years because of the lack of money for implementation of initial agreements. Additional funding will be needed from the U.N., the World Bank or other international sources, if these programs are to achieve their goals. One useful mechanism is the Global Environment Facility (GEF), which is currently funding the Black Sea regional program and a number of other smaller coastal management efforts. Part of the GEF's mission is to protect international waters, including the marine environment, and its funds can help to stimulate local and regional programs. Agenda 21 also calls for international funds for the protection of coastal waters and the oceans at large. Nonetheless, international lenders such as the World Bank continue to exert greater influence over coastal waters through their general development lending than through targeted environmental money. Thus their agriculture, water, urban planning, energy and other development projects merit consideration not only for their direct human benefits, but in light of the ecological needs of the oceans.[106]

Ultimately, reversing the decline of the oceans will take action percolating from the grassroots to the international level and filtering back down again in the form of international agreements to be given teeth by national laws and local action. The international moratorium on the use of driftnets, for instance, grew out of activism by such groups as Greenpeace, the Bering Sea Fishermen's Association, the American Oceans Campaign, and the Defenders of Wildlife, among others. The South Pacific Forum advanced the issue by banning the use, possession, and transit of driftnets longer than 2.5 kilometers in the waters and territory of these Pacific island nations—a sizable portion of the Pacific Ocean—and then requesting a U.N. moratorium on driftnetting. The U.N. general assembly passed its first resolution against driftnetting in 1989, and then renewed it in 1990 and 1991, leading to an international moratorium that went into effect on December 31, 1992.[107]

As of that date, Japan, Taiwan, Korea, France and Italy were still using driftnets over 2.5 kilometers in length. Japan and Korea have subsequently stopped, and France, under European law, is to end driftnetting by December 31, 1993. Taiwan has issued public statements that it would halt the practice, but its ships have since been spotted driftnetting off the coast of South Africa. In violation of both the U.N. and E.C., Italy continues to use 10- to 30-kilometer driftnets in the Mediterranean. On the whole, however, driftnetting has fallen off sharply. The 1,000 to 1,200 vessels that each used to lay 30- to 40-kilometer nets in the North Pacific are mostly gone. Likewise, driftnetting has ceased in the South Pacific.[108]

Grassroots organizations are replicating that kind of effort around the world to halt a wide range of environmental offenses, not only specifically for the sake of the oceans, but also for related purposes on land. To date, their efforts have been too few and too small to reverse marine degradation, but without their continued effort, the oceans would stand little chance.

We can no longer afford to act as if the oceans are limitless or unalterable. The marine environment is integrally connected with the human environment and the biosphere, and there are few human industries or activities that do not ultimately affect the oceans in one way or another. Poverty, population growth, industrial expansion and overconsumption intensify those effects. In order to restore the health of the oceans, we need to integrate those actions we take expressly to protect the marine environment with those being undertaken to achieve sustainable development worldwide.

The complex links between land and sea may make the task of protecting the oceans seem daunting, if not impossible. But it is precisely because of these links—because the oceans touch the lives of all of us—that we cannot ignore the health of the oceans if we are to protect our own place on the planet.

Notes

1. Marine fish supply and use as food source from *Marine Fisheries and the Law of the Sea: A Decade of Change*, FAO Fisheries Circular No. 853 (Rome: FAO, 1993). At approximately 70 million tons and 52 million tons per year, respectively, pork and beef production are second and third to marine fish production of 80 million tons per year, from Lester R. Brown et al., *Vital Signs* (New York: W.W. Norton & Co., 1993). Coastal tourism is a large but untallied percentage of the $1.9 trillion global tourism industry from Enzo Paci, World Tourism Organization, Madrid, private communication, October 19, 1992.

2. Quote from the foreword of the 1961 edition, Rachel Carson, *The Sea Around Us* (New York: Oxford University Press, 1991). The first edition was in 1950.

3. Estimate of inhabited space from W. Jackson Davis, "Global Aspects of Marine Pollution Policy," *Marine Policy*, May 1990. This percentage of the biosphere is determined by calculating the volume of the oceans, which are entirely occupied by life, and comparing it to the three dimensional size of land and air occupied by life. Organisms live up to 500 feet in the air and down to several feet in the ground. Water statistics from Fits van der Leeden et al., *The Water Encyclopedia* (Chelsea, Mich.: Lewis Publishers, Inc., 1990). In this paper, basic oceanographic and marine biology references include Dale E. Ingmanson and William J. Wallace, *Oceanography: An Introduction* (Belmont, Calif.: Wadsworth Publishing Company, 1985), *The New Encyclopedia Britannica: Macropedia*, volume 13, (Chicago, Ill.: Helen Hemingway Benton, Publisher, 1976), and numerous scientific articles.

4. Early ocean and atmosphere development from James F. Kasting, "Earth's Early Atmosphere," *Science*, February 12, 1993.

5. An example of possible regional climate change from Richard A. Kerr, "Even Warm Climates Get the Shivers," *Science*, July 16, 1993; higher global temperature from K. Rozanski, S.W. Fowler, and E.M. Scott, "Global Oceans Studies, the Greenhouse Effect, and Climate Change: Investigating Interconnections," *IAEA Bulletin*, February 1993.

6. Oxygen production from Davis, op. cit., note 3; alternatively, phytoplankton is estimated to account for nearly half of global photosynthesis from Martin V. Angel, "Managing Biodiversity in the Oceans" in Melvin N.A. Peterson, ed., *Diversity of Oceanic Life* (Washington, D.C.: Center for Strategic International Studies, 1992); 1000 years from Boyce Thorne-Miller, Ocean Advocates, private communication, September 28, 1993.

7. Carbon annually stored in oceans from P.D. Quay, B. Tilbrook, and C.S. Wong, "Oceanic Uptake of Fossil Fuel CO_2: Carbon-13 Evidence," *Science*, April 3, 1992; general discussion of carbon dioxide and annual release from Richard A. Kerr, "Fugitive Carbon Dioxide: It's not hiding in the Ocean," *Science*, April 3, 1992 and Eric T. Sundquist, "The Global Carbon Dioxide Budget," *Science*, February 12, 1993. The convention among atmospheric scientists is to give carbon dioxide figures in terms of carbon content, since these scientists are tracking the carbon through its entire cycle, from carbon dioxide, to organic carbon, and so on.

8. Quantities of carbon stored in oceans and terrestrial biosphere from John A. McGowan, "The Role of Oceans in Global Change and the Ecosystem Effects of Change" in *National Forum on Ocean Conservation*, proceedings of November 19-21, 1991 conference (Washington, D.C.: Smithsonian Institution, 1991).

9. *Marine Fisheries*, op. cit., note 1.

10. Boyce Thorne-Miller and John Catena, *The Living Ocean* (Washington, D.C.: Island Press, 1991).

11. Species count from "Biodiversity: Whither the Ocean?", *Currents* (newsletter of Woods Hole Oceanographic Institution, Woods Hole, Mass.), Spring 1993; James J. McCarthy, "Marine Productivity" in *National Forum on Ocean Conservation*, proceedings of November 19-21, 1991 conference (Washington, D.C.: Smithsonian Institution, 1991).

12. Elliot A. Norse, ed., *Global Marine Biological Diversity: A Strategy for Building Conservation into Decision Making* (Washington, D.C.: Island Press, 1993).

13. Scientific and medical uses from Jon Kohl, "The Ocean's Bounty: Untapped Pharmacy," *Currents* (newsletter of Woods Hole Oceanographic Institution, Woods Hole, Mass.), Spring 1993, Gregor Hodgson, "Drugs from the Sea," *Far Eastern Economic Review*, April 11, 1991, Lawrence K. Altman, "Sharks Yield Possible Weapon Against Infection," *New York Times*, February 15, 1993, and "Sea is the New Frontier for Developing Drugs," *New York Times*, November 10, 1992.

14. Productivity of coastal waters from McCarthy, "Marine Productivity," op. cit., note 11, and James J. McCarthy, private communication, October 4 and 13, 1993; percentage of area from John Ryther, "Photosynthesis and Fish Production in the Sea," *Science*, Vol. 166, 1969; continental shelf width from Michael Allaby, ed., *The Oxford Dictionary of Natural History* (New York: Oxford University Press, 1985); productivity of estuaries and wetlands from Ingmanson and Wallace, op. cit., note 3.

15. Fishing grounds corresponding with areas of marine productivity from U.S. Central Intelligence Agency, *The New Global Fishing Regime: Impact and Response* (Washington, D.C.: General Printing Office, June 1980); catch information from *Marine Fisheries*, op. cit., note 1. The region of the oceans that is 200 nautical miles from land, including islands, constitutes approximately one-third of oceans and is discussed in greater detail later in the paper.

16. Productivity from McCarthy, "Marine Productivity," op. cit., note 11 and McCarthy, private communication, op. cit., note 14.

17. Animal biomass from McCarthy, priv. comm., op. cit., note 14.

18. "Biodiversity: Whither the Ocean?" op. cit., note 11.

19. Thorne-Miller and Catena, op. cit., note 10.

20. Charles R.C. Sheppard, *A Natural History of the Coral Reef* (Poole, U.K.: Blandford Press, 1983).

21. Sources for paragraph and Table 2: Overview of marine pollution in Joint

Group of Experts on the Scientific Aspects of the Marine Environment (GESAMP), *The State of the Marine Environment*, UNEP Regional Seas Reports and Studies No.115, (Nairobi: UNEP, 1990); nutrient sources from World Resources Institute, *World Resources 1992-93* (New York: Oxford University Press, 1992); alien species from James T. Carlton and Jonathan B. Geller, "Ecological Roulette: The Global Transport of Nonindigenous Marine Organisms," *Science,* July 2, 1993; oil pollution from National Research Council, *Oil in the Sea: Inputs, Fates and Effects* (Washington, D.C.: National Academy Press, 1985): decline in oil pollution from "60% Drop in Oil Pollution Since 1981," *Maine Pollution Bulletin,* December 1990; examples of radioactive hot spots from Patrick E. Tyler, "Soviet's Secret Nuclear Dumping Raises Fears for Arctic Waters, *New York Times,* May 4, 1992, and Patrick E. Tyler, "The U.S., Too, Has Dumped Waste at Sea," *New York Times,* May 4, 1993; Paul E. Hagen, "The International Community Confronts Plastics Pollution from Ships: MARPOL Annex V and the Problem That Won't Go Away," *American University Journal of International Law and Policy,* Winter 1990.

22. "Marine Pollution from Land-based Sources: Facts and Figures," *UNEP Industry and Environment,* January - June 1992; Seto example from Jeremy Cherfas, "The Fringe of the Ocean—Under Siege from Land," *Science,* April 13, 1990.

23. Sewage sludge toxicity from Mark J. Costello and John C. Gamble, "Effects of Sewage Sludge on Marine Fish Embryos and Larvae," *Marine Environmental Research,* Vol. 33, 1992; sewage's contribution to nutrient load from World Resources Institute, op. cit., note 21.

24. Pollution and oyster catch from *The Chesapeake Bay: A Progress Report, 1990-91,* Chesapeake Executive Council, Annapolis, Maryland, August 1991; filter example from Andy Palmer, American Oceans Campaign, Washington, D.C., private communication, September 27, 1993.

25. J.J. Cole et al., "Nitrogen Loading of Rivers as a Human-Driven Process" in M.D. McDonnel and S.T.A. Pickett, eds., *Humans as Components of Ecosystems: The Ecology of Subtle Human Effects and Population Areas* (New York: Springer- Verlag, 1993).

26. .Aswan dam discussion in Adam Ben-Tuvia, "The Mediterranean Sea, Biological Aspects" in *Ecosystems of the World, Estuaries and Enclosed Seas,* Vol.26 (New York: Elsevier Scientific Publishing Company, 1983); Cole et al., op. cit., note 25.

27. Ninety-eight percent of lead, 80-99 percent PCBs, DDT, HCB and HCH, and the majority of cadmium, copper, iron, and zinc according to GESAMP, op. cit., note 21; North Sea from "Marine Pollution from Land-Based Sources," op. cit., note 22 and Fred Pearce, "North Sea Crude," *Audubon,* May-June 1993; Gulf war information from S.W. Fowler, "Pollution in the Gulf: Monitoring the Marine Environment," *IAEA Bulletin,* February 1993, and John Robinson, National Oceanic and Atmospheric Administration, Washington, D.C., private communication, October 13, 1993 (estimates for the amount directly dumped range from 4 to 12 million barrels; the 4 to 5 million barrels estimate is equally rough, and could be higher over the long term due to runoff); global oil pollution numbers from National Research Council, op. cit., note 21.

28. Examples and background from Norse, op. cit., note 12; and James T. Carlton, "Irreversible Global Invasions of Alien Species in Coastal Waters: The Deluge Grows and Grows" in *National Forum on Ocean Conservation,* proceedings of

November 19-21, 1991 conference (Washington, D.C.: Smithsonian Institution, 1991).

29. Wood ship fouling mass and red tides from Carlton, "Irreversible Global Invasions of Alien Species," op. cit., note 28; Australian results from Makoto Omori, Christopher P. Norman, and Hiroshi Yamakawa, "Biodiversity: Human Impacts through Fisheries and Transportation" in Melvin N.A. Peterson, ed., *Diversity of Oceanic Life: An Evaluative Review* (Washington, D.C.: The Center for Strategic and International Studies, 1992).

30. South Africa from "Experts say Toxic, Alien Organisms in Ballast Water," *Environmental Issues*, Foreign Broadcast Information Service, U.S. Government, April 9, 1993; United States from James T. Carlton, Maritime Studies Program, Williams College, Mystic Seaport, Conn., private communication, September 30, 1993; species in transit from Carlton and Geller, "Ecological Roulette," op. cit., note 21.

31. Norse, op. cit., note 12.

32. John Browne, "Restocking and Sea-ranching" and Lars P. Hansen, "Status of Atlantic Salmon in Norway" in *Wild Salmon—Present and Future*, proceedings of September 16 and 17, 1988, international conference, Sherkin Island, Ireland.

33. Singapore from L.M. Chou, "Singapore," *ASEAN Marine Science*, (Newsletter of the ASEAN-Australia Marine Science Project, Townsville, Australia), April 1992; San Francisco Bay from Elliot Norse, Center for Marine Conservation, private communication, April 23, 1993 and Michael A. Rozengurt, "Alternation of Freshwater Inflows" in Richard H. Stroud, ed., *Stemming the Tide of Coastal Fish Habitat Loss* (Savannah, Georgia: National Coalition for Marine Conservation, 1992); Palos Verdes from Ingmanson and Wallace, op. cit., note 3.

34. Wetland loss from World Resources Institute, op. cit., note 21; coral reef loss from Clive R. Wilkinson, "Coral Reefs are Facing Widespread Extinctions: Can We Prevent These Through Sustainable Management Practices?" presented at the Seventh International Coral Reef Symposium, Guam, 1992; beach erosion from H. Jesse Walker, "The Coastal Zone" in B.L. Turner II et al., eds., *The Earth as Transformed by Human Action* (Cambridge: Cambridge University Press, 1990). For other coastal habitat in decline see B.G. Hatcher et al., "Review of Research Relevant to the Conservation of Shallow Tropical Marine Ecosystems," *Oceanography and Marine Biology Annual Review*, Vol.27, 1989, pp.337-414 and Geoffry Lean et al., *World Wildlife Fund Atlas of the Environment* (New York: Prentice Hall Press, 1990).

35. Estimates of coastal populations vary, with 50 percent within 100 kilometers of the shoreline as a rough consensus; Southeast Asia from foreword of Chua Thia-Eng and Daniel Pauly, eds., *Coastal Area Management in Southeast Asia: Policies, Management Strategies and Case Studies* (Manila: International Center for Living Aquatic Resources Management, 1989); coastal population density in China is 312 persons per square kilometer v. the national average of 107 persons per square kilometer from Fan Zhijie and R.P. Côté, "Population, Development and Marine Pollution in China," *Marine Policy*, May 1991; regions of high coastal population density from *The Times Atlas of the World* (New York: Times Books, 1985).

36. Largest cities from Otto Johnson, ed., *The 1992 Information Please Almanac* (Boston, Mass.: Houghton Mifflin Company, 1992); Eugene Robinson, "Worldwide Migration Nears Crisis," *Washington Post*, July 7, 1993; world population in coastal cities from World Resources Institute, op. cit., note 21.

37. Rural migration information from Don Hinrichsen, presentation at Worldwatch Institute, July 16, 1993; shrimp production from *Marine Fisheries*, op. cit., note 1; Thai situation from Alfredo Quarto, Mangrove Action Project, Port Angeles, Wash., private communication, September 30, 1993 and Suvit Suvit-Sawasdi, "Perasak is not the first and will not be the last," *Bangkok Post*, April 25, 1993; general discussion in Peter Weber, "Missing Mangroves," *World Watch*, March/April 1993.

38. Marlise Simons, "A Dutch Reversal: Letting the Sea Back In," *New York Times*, March 7, 1993; *A New Coastal Defence Policy for the Netherlands* (Gravenhage, The Netherlands: Ministry of Transport and Public Works, 1990); rate of loss of Louisiana coastal wetlands from Peggy Rooney, "Louisiana's Wetlands Calamity," *EPA Journal*, September/October 1989; area of Louisiana coastal wetlands from Ralph W. Tiner, Jr., *Wetlands of the United States: Current Status and Recent Trends* (Washington, D.C.: U.S. Fish and Wildlife Service, 1984).

39. Sea level rise from Intergovernmental Panel on Climate Change (IPCC), *Climate Change: The IPCC Scientific Assessment* (New York: Cambridge University Press, 1990); beach loss from Orrin H. Pilkey, "The Shoreline Erosion Problem," *Ocean and Coastal Policy Briefing*, February 23, 1989, United States Senate, Washington, D.C., sponsored by the Oceanic Society, Environmental Policy Institute, and Friends of the Earth.

40. Agricultural diversion information from Rozengurt, op. cit., note 33; regional impounded runoff from GESAMP, op. cit., note 21.

41. Cindy Lee Van Dover et al., "Stable Isotope Evidence for Entry of Sewage-Derived Organic Material into a Deep-Sea Food Web," *Nature*, Vol.360, November 12, 1992.

42. Ocean dumping from GESAMP, op. cit., note 21. For examples of dumping military and nuclear wastes see Anthony Hubbard, "Chemical War: Our Seabed Legacy," *Listener & TV Times* (New Zealand), January 16, 1993, Fredrik Laurin, "Scandinavia's Underwater Time Bomb," *The Bulletin of the Atomic Scientists*, March 1991, Hal Bernton, "Russian Revelations Indicate Arctic Region is Awash in Contaminants," *Washington Post*, May 17, 1993, and Davis, op. cit., note 3. For proposals to use seabed for disposal site see *Feasibility of Disposal of High-Level Radioactive Waste into the Seabed*, Volume 1 (Paris: Organization for Economic Co-operation and Development, 1988), Julian M. Weiss, "Seabed Mining Offers Hope for Island Economies," *Christian Science Monitor*, May 17, 1990, W. Jackson Davis and Jon M. Van Dyke, "Dumping of Decommissioned Nuclear Submarines at Sea," *Marine Policy*, November 1990, and Bronwen Maddox, "Last Stop for Britain's Nuclear Submarines," *Financial Times*, September 28, 1992.

43. John T. Hardy, "Where the Sea Meets the Sky," *Natural History*, May 1991.

44. Snail example from Palmer, op. cit., note 24.

45. R.C. Smith et al., "Ozone Depletion: Ultraviolet Radiation and Phytoplankton

Biology in Antarctic Waters," *Science*, February 12, 1992; John Hardy and Hermann Gucinski, "Stratospheric Ozone Depletion: Implications for Marine Ecosystems," *Oceanography*, November 1989.

46. Scientific consensus predictions for global warming from IPCC, op. cit., note 39, updated in IPCC, *Climate Change 1992* (New York: Cambridge University Press, 1992); Peter W. Glynn, "Coral Reef Bleaching in the 1980s and Possible Connections with Global Warming," *Trends in Ecology and Evolution*, June 1991; Little Ice Age from Walter Sullivan, "Study of Greenland Ice Finds Rapid Change in Past Climates," *New York Times*, July 15, 1993 and Kathy Sawyer, "Climatology: Warming Could Trigger Cold Spells," *Washington Post*, July 19, 1993.

47. Maryland Sea Grant College, *Workshop on Coral Bleaching, Coral Reef Ecosystems and Global Change: Report of Proceedings* held in Miami, Florida, June 17-21, 1991.

48. Norse, op. cit., note 12.

49. Sources for paragraph and Table 3: Extinctions from Norse, op. cit., note 12, and David Day, *The Doomsday Book of Animals: A Natural History for Vanished Species* (New York: Viking Press, 1981); trends from Ed Ayres, "Many Marine Mammal Populations Declining," *Vital Signs 1993* (New York: W.W. Norton & Co., 1993).

50. J.W. Copland and J.S. Lucas, eds., *Giant Clams in Asia and the Pacific* (Canberra: Australian Centre for International Agricultural Research, 1988).

51. Net sizes from David E. Pitt, "Despite Gaps, Data Leave Little Doubt That Fish Are in Peril," *New York Times*, August 3, 1993.

52. Decline in cod, etc. and global trends from *Marine Fisheries*, op. cit., note 1; "Canada Warns of Action Over Fishing," *Journal of Commerce*, November 20, 1992; "Canada, Europe Agree to Oppose Overfishing," *Journal of Commerce*, December 22, 1992.

53. Historical trend from Ray Hilborn, "Marine Biota" in B.L. Turner II et al., eds., *The Earth as Transformed by Human Action* (Cambridge: Cambridge University Press, 1990); recent global trends and Peruvian example from *Marine Fisheries*, op. cit., note 1; population growth from U.N. Department of International Economic and Social Affairs, *World Population Prospects 1988* (New York: 1989); 1990s data from FAO Fisheries Department, "Global Fish and Shellfish Production in 1991," COFI Support Document: Fishery Statistics, Rome, March 1993 and John Madeley, "Law of Diminishing Returns Hits World Fish Catch," *Financial Times*, June 17, 1993.

54. *Marine Fisheries*, op. cit., note 1.

55. *Marine Fisheries*, op. cit., note 1.

56. Fishery status from Pitt, op. cit., note 51; quote from *Marine Fisheries*, op. cit., note 1.

57. One hundred million ton estimate from the FAO sponsored publication J.A. Gulland, ed., *The Fish Resources of the Ocean* (Surrey, England: Fishing News Ltd., 1971). This estimate is meant to include traditional boney fish ranging from commonly eaten species such as cod and haddock to the small shoaling species such as the Peruvian anchovy. Current FAO projections from *Marine Fisheries*, op. cit., note 1.

58. Driftnet bycatch from Palmer, op. cit., note 24; purse seine dolphin catch from Eric Christensen and Samantha Geffin, "GATT Sets Its Nets on Environmental Regulation: The GATT Panel Ruling on Mexican Yellowfin Tuna Imports and the Need for Reform of the International Trading System," *The University of Miami Inter-American Law Review*, Winter 1991-92 and Hillary F. French, "The Tuna Test: GATT and the Environment," *World Watch*, March/April 1992.

59. Because bycatch is undocumented, estimates vary widely. The total bycatch from shrimp in developing countries is estimated to be 10 to 15 million tons per year in Basil Hinds, "The Economics of Fish Resources in Lesser Developed Countries: The Fish By-Catch and Externalities in Shrimp Fishery," PhD Dissertation, Howard University, 1981 cited in Lennox Hinds, "World Marine Fisheries," *Marine Policy*, September 1992. Shrimp bycatch estimated at 4.5 to 19 million tons per year with one-quarter to one-half discarded while the total bycatch is estimated at 9 million tons per year in Eugene C. Bricklemyer, Jr., Suzanne Iudicello, and Hans J. Hartmann, "Discarded Catch in U.S. Commercial Marine Fisheries" in William J. Chandler, *Audubon Wildlife Report 1989/1990* (New York: Academic Press, Inc., 1989). FAO estimates that 80 to 90 percent of the shrimp catch in the tropics is bycatch in *Marine Fisheries*, op. cit., note 1.

60. *Marine Fisheries*, op. cit., note 1.

61. Sand eel from Mark Avery and Rhys Green, "Not Enough Fish in the Sea," *New Scientist*, July 22, 1989; David Cameron Duffy, "Environmental Uncertainty and Commercial Fishing: Effects on Peruvian Guano Birds," *Biological Conservation*, Vol.26, 1983, pp.227-238; pollack from Natalia S. Mirovitskaya and J. Christopher Haney, "Fisheries Exploitation as a Threat to Environmental Security: The North Pacific Ocean," *Marine Policy*, July 1992; Tim MacClanahan, "Triggerfish: Coral Reef Keystone Predator," *Swara* (East African Wildlife Society, Nairobi, Kenya), May/June 1992.

62. Han J. Lindeboom, "How Trawlers are Raking the North Sea to Death," *The Daily Telegraph*, March 19, 1990.

63. Lindeboom, op. cit., note 62.

64. Omori et al., op. cit., note 29.

65. Total employment from Lennox Hinds, "World Marine Fisheries," *Marine Policy*, September 1992; 50,000 from Mark Clayton, "Hunt for Jobs Intensifies as Fishing Industry Implodes," *Christian Science Monitor*, August 25, 1993; "French Lose Out on Fish Ban," *Down to Earth*, May 15, 1993; conflict between trawlers and small-scale fishers from Hinrichsen, presentation, op. cit., note 37.

66. John Kurien, *Ruining the Commons and Responses of the Commoners: Coastal Overfishing and Fishermen's Actions in Kerala State, India*, Discussion Paper 23 (Geneva: U.N. Research Institute for Social Development, May 1991); J.M. Vakily, "Assessing and Managing the Marine Fish Resources of Sierra Leone, West Africa," *Naga, The ICLARM Quarterly* (Manila), January 1992.

67. Price from *Marine Fisheries*, op. cit., note 1; fish consumption per capita from FAO, *1991 Yearbook of Fishery Statistics: Commodities* (Rome: 1993); Paul Reeves, "Fish Slips from the Poor Man's Table," *ICLARM Newsletter*, Manila, April 1985; Kelly Haggart, "Exporting More, Eating Less," *Panoscope*, November 1992.

68. *Muro-ami* from Gregor Hodgson, "Bubble Bath for Coral," *Far Eastern Economic Review*, March 7, 1991; "employer of last resort" from *Marine Fisheries*, op. cit., note 1; coastward migration from Hinrichsen, presentation, op. cit., note 37; aquaculture environmental implications also in Hal Kane, "Growing Fish in Fields," *World Watch*, September/October 1993.

69. *Marine Fisheries*, op. cit., note 1. One nautical mile is equal to 1.15 English miles or 1.85 kilometers.

70. History of the Law of the Sea from Clyde Sanger, *Ordering the Oceans: The Making of the Law of the Sea* (London: Zed Books, 1986); actual text in *The Law of the Sea* (New York: United Nations, 1983).

71. *The Law of the Sea*, op. cit., note 70.

72. *The Law of the Sea*, op. cit., note 70; 39 countries from Tullio Treves, "Oceans" in T. Scovazzi and T. Treves, eds., *World Treaties for the Protection of the Environment* (Milano: Istituto per L'Ambiente, 1992).

73. Ratification by Malta in May of 1993 brought the total count to 57 from Mark LaBell, United Nations Office of Legal Affairs, private communication, September 22, 1993. Over 120 countries signed the final test in 1983, but unlike signing a contract, signing an international treaty is not binding. Ratification is when a country actually agrees to implement and abide by a treaty.

74. Change in status of the Law of the Sea from Rita J. Diehl, international oceans law lawyer, Falls Church, Virginia, private communication, September 22, 1993; draft of changes from circulation document labeled: United Nations Convention on Law of the Sea, Draft Resolution for Adoption by the General Assembly, August 3, 1993.

75. "60% Drop in Oil Pollution Since 1981," op. cit., note 21; London Dumping Convention from Davis, op. cit., note 3 and "Agreement Reached on Dumping at Sea," *Journal of Commerce*, November 16, 1992.

76. "IMO to Study Ballast Water Introductions," *Marine Pollution Bulletin*, December 1990.

77. Seventy signatories from Treves, op. cit., note 72.

78. Example of plastics and other ship wastes from Hagen, op. cit., note 21.

79. William P. Coughlin, "Illegal Disposal of Toxic Wastes From Ships Seen Global Occurrence," *Journal of Commerce*, March 5, 1991; U.S. and Norway example from Hagen, op. cit., note 21.

80. U.N. negotiations from David E. Pitt, "U.N. Talks Combat Threat to Fishery," *New York Times*, July 25, 1993 and Palmer, op. cit., note 24; Agenda 21 fishing provisions from *Report of the United Nations Conference on Environment and Development (UNCED)*, Rio de Janeiro, June 3-14, 1992 (August 13, 1992 version).

81. Sealing treaty from *Marine Fisheries*, op. cit., note 1.

82. T.R. Ried, "World Whaling Body Riven by Dispute," *Washington Post*, May 15, 1993; Andrew Pollack, "They Eat Whales, Don't They?" *New York Times*, May 3, 1993; Karen Fossil, "Defiant Oslo approves Whale Hunt," *Financial Times*, May 19, 1993; minke populations from "Saving the Whale," *Financial Times*, May 17, 1993; Norwegian whale kill from Rick Atkinson, "Oslo Stands Firm on Whales," *Washington Post*, October 1, 1993.

83. UNCED, op. cit., note 80; Montreal Guidelines from "Marine Pollution from Land-Based Sources," op. cit., note 22.

84. Traditional fishing systems from Gary A. Klee, "Oceania," in Gary A. Klee, ed., *World Systems of Traditional Resource Management* (New York: John Wiley & Sons, 1980), R.E. Johannes, CSIRO Marine Laboratories, Australia, "Small- Scale Fisheries: A Storehouse of Knowledge for Managing Coastal Marine Resources" in *National Forum on Ocean Conservation*, proceedings of November 19-21, 1991 conference (Washington, D.C.: Smithsonian Institution, 1991), Conner Bailey, Auburn University, Auburn, Ala., and Charles Zerner, Woodrow Wilson Institution, Washington, D.C., "Role of Traditional Fisheries Resource Management Systems for Sustainable Resource Utilization," presented at Perikanan Dalam Pembangunan Jangka Panjang Tahap II: Tantangan dan Peluang, Sukabumi, West Java, June 18-21, 1991. Decline of traditional Pacific Island systems from Michael Gawel, Territorial Planning Office of Guam, private communication, August 20, 1992.

85. A. Caverivière, "Bigger Net Mesh Size Will Mean Bigger Catches in the Ivory Coast Trawl Fishery," *Naga, The ICLARM Quarterly*, Manila, July 1986.

86. W. Ballantine, "Marine Reserves for New Zealand," *University of Aukland, Leigh Laboratory Bulletin*, No.25, pp.1-196, 1991.

87. Vakily, op. cit., note 66.

88. Philippine example from Hinrichsen, presentation, op. cit., note 37; see also, Don Hinrichsen, "Philippine Mangroves: Bounty in the Brine," *International Wildlife*, May/June 1992, "Managing Mangroves in the Philippines," *People*, November 3, 1991, and Weber, op. cit., note 37.

89. *Marine Fisheries*, op. cit., note 1.

90. Australia example from *Marine Fisheries*, op. cit., note 1.

91. *Marine Fisheries*, op. cit., note 1.

92. Krill limit from Stephen Nicol and William de la Mare, "Ecosystem Management and the Antarctic Krill," *American Scientist*, January-February 1993; discussion of shortcomings of CCAMLR in Norse, op. cit., note 12; sustainability discussed by Donald Ludwig, Ray Hilborn, and Carl Walters, "Uncertainty, Resource Exploitation, and Conservation: Lessons from History," *Science*, April 2, 1993.

93. Netherlands from Simons, op. cit., note 38 and *A New Coastal Defence Policy*, op. cit., note 38.

94. Predicted effects of global warming from IPCC, op. cit., note 39 and IPCC, op. cit., note 46.

95. Donald D. Robadue, Jr., Coastal Resources Center, University of Rhode Island, private communication, September 27, 1993; Donald D. Robadue, Jr., and Luis Arriaga, "Ecuador's Coastal Resources Management Program", *Intercoast Network*, (Narragansett, Rhode Island: Coastal Resources Center, University of Rhode Island) Spring 1993.

96. Coastal tourism from Edward D. Goldberg, "Competitors for Coastal Ocean Space," *Oceanus*, Spring 1993; Sirikul Bunpapong and Apiradee Ngernvijit, "Coral Reef Management Plan for the Islands of Ban Don Bay, Thailand" in Chou Loke Ming et al., eds., *Towards an Integrated Management of Tropical Resources* (Manila: International Center for Living Aquatic Resources Management, 1991).

97. Wendy Craik, Great Barrier Reef Marine Park Authority, "The Great Barrier Reef Marine Park: Its Establishment, Development and Current Status" (draft), June 1992.

98. Craik, op. cit., note 97.

99. GESAMP, op. cit., note 21.

100. For further discussion of waste water and other water issues, see Sandra Postel, *Last Oasis: Facing Water Scarcity* (New York: W.W. Norton & Co., 1992).

101. For a discussion of the reduction of industrial waste water, see Postel, op. cit., note 100.

102. Size of Chesapeake watershed, 166,000 square kilometers, from Christopher F. D'Elia, "Too Much of a Good Thing: Nutrient Enrichment of the Chesapeake Bay," *Environment*, March 1987; agreement provisions from *The Chesapeake Bay*, op. cit., note 24.

103. *The Chesapeake Bay*, op. cit., note 24.

104. "Marine Pollution from Land-Based Sources," op. cit., note 22; Don Hinrichsen, *Our Common Seas: Coasts in Crisis* (London: Earthscan, 1990); World Resources Institute, op. cit., note 21; M. K. Tolba and O. A. El-Kholy, eds., *The World Environment 1972-1992: Two Decades of Change* (New York: Chapman & Hall, 1992).

105. Hinrichsen, *Our Common Seas*, op. cit., note 104.

106. GEF involvement in the Black Sea from "Black Sea Nations Join Battle Against Pollution," *World Bank News*, July 22, 1993; GEF mission from Ian Johnson, "Cross-Sectorial Issues Affecting Land-Based Pollution," *Marine Policy*, January 1992; for funding recommendations see UNCED, op. cit., note 80.

107. "South Pacific Forum: Final Act of the Meeting on a Convention to Prohibit Driftnet Fishing in the South Pacific, Including Text of Convention for the Prohibition of Fishing with Long Driftnets in the South Pacific and its Protocols (November 24, 1989)," *International Legal Materials*, Vol.XXIX, No.6, p.1449, November 1990; first U.N. resolution against driftnets from "United Nations: General Assembly Resolution on *Large-Scale Pelagic Driftnet Fishing* *and Its Impact on Living Marine Resources of the World's Oceans and Seas* (passed December 22, 1989)," *International Legal Materials*, Vol.XXIX, No.6, p.1555, November 1990; 1990 and 1991 U.N. resolutions from Mike Hagler, Greenpeace International, Devonport, Auckland, Australia, private communication, October 1, 1993.

108. Status of driftnetting from Hagler, op. cit., note 107, and Gerald Leape, Greenpeace, Washington, D.C., private communication, October 13, 1993.

THE WORLDWATCH PAPER SERIES

_____ 100. **Beyond the Petroleum Age: Designing a Solar Economy** by Christopher Flavin and Nicholas Lenssen.
_____ 101. **Discarding the Throwaway Society** by John E. Young.
_____ 102. **Women's Reproductive Health: The Silent Emergency** by Jodi L. Jacobson.
_____ 103. **Taking Stock: Animal Farming and the Environment** by Alan B. Durning and Holly B. Brough.
_____ 104. **Jobs in a Sustainable Economy** by Michael Renner.
_____ 105. **Shaping Cities: The Environmental and Human Dimensions** by Marcia D. Lowe.
_____ 106. **Nuclear Waste: The Problem That Won't Go Away** by Nicholas Lenssen.
_____ 107. **After the Earth Summit: The Future of Environmental Governance** by Hilary F. French.
_____ 108. **Life Support: Conserving Biological Diversity** by John C. Ryan.
_____ 109. **Mining the Earth** by John E. Young.
_____ 110. **Gender Bias: Roadblock to Sustainable Development** by Jodi L. Jacobson.
_____ 111. **Empowering Development: The New Energy Equation** by Nicholas Lenssen.
_____ 112. **Guardians of the Land: Indigenous Peoples and the Health of the Earth** by Alan Thein Durning.
_____ 113. **Costly Tradeoffs: Reconciling Trade and the Environment** by Hilary F. French.
_____ 114. **Critical Juncture: The Future of Peacekeeping** by Michael Renner.
_____ 115. **Global Network: Computers in a Sustainable Society** by John E. Young.
_____ 116. **Abandoned Seas: Reversing the Decline of the Oceans** by Peter Weber.

_____ **Total Copies**

☐ **Single Copy: $5.00**
☐ **Bulk Copies (any combination of titles)**
    ☐ 2–5: $4.00 ea.   ☐ 6–20: $3.00 ea.   ☐ 21 or more: $2.00 ea.

☐ **Membership in the Worldwatch Library: $25.00 (international airmail $40.00)**
The paperback edition of our 250-page "annual physical of the planet," *State of the World 1993*, plus all Worldwatch Papers released during the calendar year.

☐ **Subscription to *World Watch* Magazine: $15.00 (international airmail $30.00)**
Stay abreast of global environmental trends and issues with our award-winning, eminently readable bimonthly magazine.

No postage required on prepaid orders. Minimum $3 postage and handling charge on unpaid orders.

Make check payable to Worldwatch Institute
1776 Massachusetts Avenue, N.W., Washington, D.C. 20036-1904 USA

Enclosed is my check for U.S. $_____

_____

name   **daytime phone #**

_____

address

_____

city   **state**   **zip/country**